Praise for *The Nine Type of Difficult People*

T0286861

'A real gem of a book, full of clear, insightful and practical advice on how to deal with difficult people in a caring and effective manner.'
Bridget Caldwell, BAFTA and double Royal Television Society award-winning director and producer

'Compelling reading for anyone leading people. The book offers a practical, easy-to-understand framework, which will help you diagnose, address and resolve problems.'
Phil Jones MBE, Managing Director, Brother UK, an Investors in People Platinum award-winning employer

'I have agonised about certain individuals and what they are doing to upset a high performing team. A book that should be on hand for any leader.'
Tony Attard OBE DL, Chairman, Panaz Group; Master of The Furniture Makers' Company (City of London livery company); past High Sheriff of Lancashire

'Not every difficult person is the same or can be managed in the same way. Nick gives you tools to identify, understand and maximise their value.'
Ian Dormer CBE (awarded for contribution to business); Chartered Director (CDir), HonFIoD; Managing Director, Rosh Engineering Ltd

'An excellent self-help book as well as an important one to help leaders and managers understand team dynamics.'
Hilary Sutcliffe, Carnegie Centre Advisory Board Member; DAVOS workshop facilitator; Director of Society Inside

The 9 Types of Difficult People

Pearson

At Pearson, we have a simple mission: to help people make more of their lives through learning.

We combine innovative learning technology with trusted content and educational expertise to provide engaging and effective learning experiences that serve people wherever and whenever they are learning.

From classroom to boardroom, our curriculum materials, digital learning tools and testing programmes help to educate millions of people worldwide – more than any other private enterprise.

Every day our work helps learning flourish, and wherever learning flourishes, so do people.

To learn more, please visit us at **www.pearson.com**

The 9 Types of Difficult People

How to spot them and quickly improve working relationships

Nick Robinson

Pearson

Harlow, England • London • New York • Boston • San Francisco • Toronto • Sydney
Dubai • Singapore • Hong Kong • Tokyo • Seoul • Taipei • New Delhi
Cape Town • São Paulo • Mexico City • Madrid • Amsterdam • Munich • Paris • Milan

PEARSON EDUCATION LIMITED
KAO Two
KAO Park
Harlow CM17 9NA
United Kingdom
Tel: +44 (0)1279 623623
Web: www.pearson.com

ISBN: 978-1-292-72606-9 (print)
           978-1-292-45778-9 (ePub)

British Library Cataloguing-in-Publication Data
A catalogue record for the print edition is available from the British Library

Library of Congress Cataloging-in-Publication Data
Names: Robinson, Nick (Executive coach), author.
Title: The 9 types of difficult people : how to spot them and quickly
    improve working relationships / Nick Robinson.
Other titles: Nine types of difficult people
Description: First edition. | Harlow, England ; New York : Pearson, 2023. |
    Includes bibliographical references and index.
Identifiers: LCCN 2023036082 | ISBN 9781292726069 (hardcover) | ISBN
    9781292457789 (epub)
Subjects: LCSH: Psychology, Industrial. | Industrial sociology. | Typology
    (Psychology)
Classification: LCC HF5548.8 .R576 2023 | DDC 158.7--dc23/eng/20230811
LC record available at https://lccn.loc.gov/2023036082

10 9 8 7 6 5 4 3 2 1
27 26 25 24 23

Cover design by Kelly Miller

Print edition typeset in 10/14 Charter ITC Pro by Straive

NOTE THAT ANY PAGE CROSS REFERENCES REFER TO THE PRINT EDITION

Contents

___

Contents

Pearson's Commitment to Diversity, Equity and Inclusion

Pearson is dedicated to creating bias-free content that reflects the diversity, depth and breadth of all learners' lived experiences. We embrace the many dimensions of diversity including, but not limited to, race, ethnicity, gender, sex, sexual orientation, socioeconomic status, ability, age and religious or political beliefs.

Education is a powerful force for equity and change in our world. It has the potential to deliver opportunities that improve lives and enable economic mobility. As we work with authors to create content for every product and service, we acknowledge our responsibility to demonstrate inclusivity and incorporate diverse scholarship so that everyone can achieve their potential through learning. As the world's leading learning company, we have a duty to help drive change and live up to our purpose to help more people create a better life for themselves and to create a better world.

Our ambition is to purposefully contribute to a world where:

- Everyone has an equitable and lifelong opportunity to succeed through learning.
- Our educational products and services are inclusive and represent the rich diversity of learners.
- Our educational content accurately reflects the histories and lived experiences of the learners we serve.
- Our educational content prompts deeper discussions with students and motivates them to expand their own learning and worldview.

We are also committed to providing products that are fully accessible to all learners. As per Pearson's guidelines for accessible educational Web media, we test and retest the capabilities of our products against the highest standards for every release, following the WCAG guidelines in developing new products for copyright year 2022 and beyond. You can learn more about Pearson's commitment to accessibility at:

https://www.pearson.com/us/accessibility.html

While we work hard to present unbiased, fully accessible content, we want to hear from you about any concerns or needs regarding this Pearson product so that we can investigate and address them.

- Please contact us with concerns about any potential bias at: https://www.pearson.com/report-bias.html
- For accessibility-related issues, such as using assistive technology with Pearson products, alternative text requests, or accessibility documentation, email the Pearson Disability Support team at: disability.support@pearson.com

About the author

———

Nick Robinson has been an executive coach since 1999. He works with leaders and managers in large and small businesses and organisations in the private, public and third sectors.

Nick has both hard- and soft-skills qualifications. He is a former Chartered Accountant (FCCA) with an MBA, awarded with Commendation, from Bayes Business School, London. Additionally, he is a Certified Professional Coach, an NLP Master Practitioner and a graduate of the Newfield Mastery in Coaching Programme.

Previously he worked in senior roles in Finance, Corporate Strategy, and held the role of Project Director and other operational roles in one of the UK's largest organisations. Nick also set up and grew a small international consultancy business. He was elected for two terms to the National Governing Council of the Institute of Directors (IoD), having previously served on their Regional Board and before that as chair of the Cheshire County Branch. Nick has also served two terms as a Non-Executive Director and Chair of Audit on the board of an NHS Hospital Trust.

For over 20 years, Nick's coaching work has centred on helping leaders and managers to navigate challenging situations and manage difficult relationships at work. His approach is designed to understand and enhance his clients' natural strengths. It addresses common concerns, such as boosting confidence, managing workload pressures, stepping up to high-profile leadership roles, and navigating the sometimes tricky dynamics of team relationships.

Nick began blogging early in his coaching career, mostly as a way to make sense of the patterns and issues that emerged in his practice. This led to commissions by two corporate clients to write management booklets, which he later self-published. This writing experience, coupled with his dealings with one particular 'difficult person' in his coaching practice, shaped the impetus for this book.

Publisher's acknowledgements

———

3 Henry Ford: Quoted by Henry Ford; **13** Socrates: Quoted by Socrates; **23** Jesse Jackson: Quoted by Jesse Jackson; **29** Peter Drucker: Quoted by Peter Drucker; **33** Stephen Covey: Quoted by Stephen Covey; **41** Albert Szent-Gyorgyi: Quoted by Albert Szent-Gyorgyi; **49** Rami Shapiro: Quoted by Rami Shapiro; **55** Thomas Paine: Quoted by Thomas Paine; **63** G.K. Chesterton: Quoted by G.K. Chesterton; **69** Steve Martin: Quoted by Steve Martin; **85** Mike Tyson: Quoted by Mike Tyson; **103** Lao Tzu: Quoted by Lao Tzu; **119** Bertold Brecht: Quoted by Bertold Brecht; **135** Che Guevara: Quoted by Che Guevara; **151** Ted Turner: Quoted by Ted Turner; **157** John F. Kennedy: Speech by John F. Kennedy; **169** Aristotle: Quoted by Aristotle; **185** Henry Kissinger: Quoted by Henry Kissinger; **203** David Morrison: Quoted by David Morrison; **216** David Morrison: Quoted by David Morrison; **221** Eleanor Roosevelt: Quoted by Eleanor Roosevelt; **227** Francis of Assisi: Quoted by Francis of Assisi.

part 1

chapter 1

Why you need this book to deal with difficult people

'Coming together is a beginning;
keeping together is progress; working
together is success.'

Henry Ford[1]

Ground zero

About 12 years ago I was asked to coach someone who was just a few steps away from losing their job. A senior leader in a large organisation, this person was described as 'extremely difficult, scary and obstructive'. I was told that because of them the department was haemorrhaging staff and managers, important changes were being blocked, and that work and clients were suffering.

The exasperated human resources manager who commissioned me didn't expect too much but wanted to do all they should before 'pressing the nuclear button' for dismissal. I couldn't speak to this person's director – they were off sick due to the stress of dealing with it. Everyone I did speak to painted the same bleak picture.

I was intrigued by how things had got to such a place. A senior professional, with a long-standing career, in a sophisticated organisation with established standards of behaviour. All seeming to have gone so wrong. By the time our first coaching session came around I was expecting to meet something of a monster.

But what I found was very different.

It seemed to me that here was a baffled and bewildered person. Someone in a demanding role, in challenging and shifting circumstances, trying their best to get good outcomes for their department's clients. In the only way that they knew how.

As well as a slight concern that I was being played by this person, I left with lots of questions. How could there possibly be such a massive gap between what I thought – and the hugely negative experiences that other people were having? In the end, we coached together for six months and created some terrific changes in how this person approached their work and their relationships.

I then became very curious about those kinds of circumstances and started to take on more coaching work with 'difficult people'. I wondered how you could be sure to help those people and what was important for the people around them to know as they dealt with the impacts. This book is the result.

A call to action

Work is important to us because, when done right, it's where we can thrive: Doing something fulfilling alongside like-minded people. We need to be stretched by the right level of challenge: too little and we stagnate; too much and we risk overwhelm and isolation. But, work shouldn't consume our entire lives, as that can also lead to an unhealthy imbalance.

The ideal path involves work with the proper level of challenge, the right kind of community, and a suitable contribution to overall balance. Yet, when circumstances and behavioural habits knock someone off that path, they become difficult, causing everyone to suffer, not just individuals. Because organisations can consistently deliver great products and services only when their people and teams are effective and fulfilled – a tough feat with a difficult person around.

So, it is in our collective interest to be alert and curious to the possibility of a difficult person at work. Then we should ask: Why has this happened? What's going on in the wider system that's contributing to this? How do we support those who are impacted, to deal with it effectively and compassionately? And how do we help a difficult person to regain their path? The answers I've discovered so far are in this book.

Note

1 Ford, Henry (n.d.), as cited in Muñoz, John P, 'Coming together, keeping together, working together', *Peoria Magazine*, 2010. Last accessed 22 June 2023.

chapter 2

How to use this book

'One who is outside their door
has the hardest part of their journey
behind them.'

Dutch proverb

If you're dealing with a difficult person at work – as their leader, colleague or team member, or as a supportive human resources professional – this book is for you. It answers common questions about why people become difficult and gives hands-on strategies for quickly improving workplace relationships.

Part one

The first part of this book lays the groundwork for dealing with a difficult person.

Chapters 3 and 4 provide the context for why things go wrong and what signs you should look out for to confirm that you've got a difficult person at work.

Difficult though is not the same as *Different*. The arguments for encouraging all kinds of difference at work are strong and not just from a moral standpoint. We know, for example, that diverse teams outperform more homogenous ones in the longer term. Difference can and should be reasonably accommodated. Use Chapter 4 to help spot the signs that someone has become intolerably *difficult*. This is the first step in understanding how to stop accommodating and begin changing that.

Chapters 5, 6 and 7 introduce my Matrix of Difficult People, together with a quiz to help identify types and a top-level summary of each. In those chapters, and throughout this book, I'm taking the stance suggested by recent research that our personalities are not set in stone. That how we perceive and respond to the world around us (our traits) are perhaps more like skills we can learn and develop.

Chapter 8 sets out useful preparation in the form of dynamic operating principles to help adopt the best mindset and Chapter 9 presents a Visual Flowchart. Use the flowchart as a checklist to help make sure you're not missing anything and are ready for the next steps.

Throughout Part one and Part two, I've made use of metaphor, both to boost understanding and help you to then communicate your discoveries to others. For example, one sign of a difficult person is that you might feel like you're on shaky ground. Or you might notice that a normally rock-like person has become totally and silently immovable. You'll also find plenty of examples and short illustrations of what might be going on, together with a 'prepare then act' method for setting out tips and strategies that you can confidently put into practice.

Part two

Part two offers practical strategies and tactics for dealing with a difficult person and quickly improving working relationships.

Each chapter considers one of the nine types of difficult people in depth.

The chapters start with a sketch of that type in a nutshell and provide a detailed description of what they can be like at their best and what happens when things get difficult. They also give further tips on how to spot that type, concentrating on the impacts they might be having.

Each chapter has sections which focus on how to deal with a difficult person depending on whether you're a leader, team member or colleague or looking for growth tips. It's worth covering each of those sections so that you have the best context of what needs to be done and the widest range of tactics to deploy.

Chapter 19 briefly considers the rare much-more-than-difficult people. Chapter 20 gives a summary and conclusion and chapter 21 provides links to more information and online resources, including video tutorials, downloads and an interactive version of my type quiz.

Choice of approach

I hope you'll find the whole of this book useful and it is written so that it builds into a practical resource. Depending on your immediate needs, you can read from start to finish or jump in at a couple of different points, as I've suggested below. Wherever you start, you can always come back to the first few chapters whenever you want to deepen your understanding or discover a different way to unlock new approaches. Here's where to start:

Complete

Suitable if you want to get a real-world understanding of:

- Why people become difficult at work
- How to tell what 'difficult' is
- How to identify types; and
- A structured approach to dealing with specific difficult people and improving working relationships in general.

Continue on from this point to Chapter 3: Why things go wrong at work.

Urgent problem

Suitable if you've:

- Identified a specific difficult person who you need to deal with urgently; and
- Got a deep understanding of which behaviours are most problematic.

Start by using Chapter 7: Summary of types and match the behaviours described there with what you're experiencing to confirm a type. Continue forwards from there.

Hybrid

Suitable if you're:

- Aware that someone is being difficult enough for it to be a problem; but
- Not sure what it is they're saying or doing that is causing those problems; and

- Still wanting to get on and deal with things quickly.

Start with Chapter 5, using my Matrix of Difficult People to help get a handle on what can often cause a tough situation to become difficult. And continue forwards from there.

> If you get stuck or feel uncertain, use the Visual Flowchart in Chapter 9 as a checklist to make sure you're not missing anything and are prepared for the next steps.

In the next chapter we'll look at why things go wrong at work, considering the perfect storm of four factors that can each contribute to somebody being experienced as difficult.

chapter 3

Why things go wrong at work

'The secret of change is to focus all of your energy not on fighting the old, but on building the new.'

Socrates[1]

Introduction

In this chapter, we'll look at the perfect storm of factors that contribute to somebody being experienced as difficult at work.

A very common question, often posed right at the start of an assignment to coach somebody who is described as difficult at work, is: 'Why has this happened?'

Leaders are usually already asking themselves that question, even before they put it out loud to me as part of our briefing process. They want to know if something they've done has created a bad situation. And they want to know how to fix it.

The individuals affected are also likely to be thinking about it, if slightly differently. They often want to know if there's something wrong with them for having fallen into this in the first place.

Understanding why someone might become difficult at work is useful for two main reasons.

First, because it can help to find useful routes to positive change. When we examine the causes, people usually see that it will help if they move beyond that question of whether or not they did something wrong, or whether or not there's something wrong with them. Instead, it helps to focus forwards on to how things could be once we're over a rough patch and out of the difficulty.

Second, it can help build a kind of managerial emotional intelligence in the organisation. The ability to understand and adapt to people and situations. That ability is both a vital skill set for everybody and a possibly useful way of uncovering whether some of the causes might also be structural, that is, in the way the organisation itself operates.

The rest of this chapter considers the perfect storm of factors that contribute to somebody being experienced as difficult at work.

Each of these alone is probably not sufficient and it's when they overlap, possibly three or four at a time, that things go awry.
The factors are:

1 Leadership lapses – when there are a number of missing, unaddressed or mismatched leadership functions

2 Turbulent times – when the organisation faces substantial change and uncertainty

3 Comfort zone breaches – when people have been too far or too long outside their comfort zones

4 The dimensions of the Matrix of Difficult People – when over-reliance on stress strategies and inflexibility of attention focus causes problems.

Leadership lapses

Good leadership is tough to do.

Leaders have to bring together disparate groups of people, inspire them with a compelling vision of the future, balance out long-term competitive strategy with short-term priorities, overcome obstacles, and cope with setbacks – and all with limited resources.

According to many experts, leadership is also getting tougher, as leaders now need to deal with the increased pace of techno-logical change and the need to innovate products and services much faster than before. As leadership guru John Kotter recently wrote in Harvard Business School's *Working Knowledge*, leaders now need to head up both traditional hierarchies that can exploit the business' core markets *and* guide and inspire loose coalitions of innovative, networked people who can create much-needed new opportunities.[2] I think that takes some serious organisational and people skills.

Against that background and with those often competing demands, it's no surprise that occasionally there are lapses in our ideal kind of leadership which might contribute to somebody becoming difficult at work. Here are the crucial ones:

Communication

This seems to occur when either the *level* of communication that a leader has or the leader's communication *style* doesn't match what their individual team member needs.

Here's a couple of key examples that I notice a lot:

- **Unmet needs for recognition** – some people need to be told when they're doing a good job, while others don't.
- **Mismatch of reasoning styles** – some people just don't find their leader's communication style convincing. Perhaps because it focuses on problems rather than on opportunities, or it stresses using tried-and-tested approaches rather than innovative ones.

Being unaware of (or inflexible about) communication style and level seems to have an impact on whether or not someone becomes more difficult over time.

Co-ordination and planning

One of the most important functions of leadership is bringing people together and uniting them with both a compelling vision of the future and a clear sense of how to balance short-term needs with long-term strategy. I've seen several people get into difficulty at work because their leaders *haven't* done the following critical things:

- Set clear priorities, so that they can square the competing demands of their immediate tasks vs. the development work that's needed for the long-term vision.
- Involved them in developing that vision, so they can understand it and own it.
- Turned strategy into actions, so that there's a visible set of projects that everybody knows will deliver that vision.

Elephants in the room

The point about elephants is that they're big. If leaders avoid discussing and dealing with the issues they represent then, over time, there's very little space left for anything else.

We all know they're there, but if we have to squeeze past them all the time, our attention, energy, concerns and worries become focused on not mentioning them and not getting squashed by the elephants.

In my experience, a room full of elephants makes it easier for somebody to fall into the trap of getting described as difficult at work – and not dealing with the elephants is a significant leadership lapse.

Turbulent times

Businesses or organisations often face turbulence in their operating environment, characterised by change and uncertainty and these will inevitably affect the people in them.

For example, the American Psychological Association's recent annual well-being survey found that half of the national workforce would be affected by organisational changes in the survey year. The same survey also found that those undergoing change were more than twice as likely to experience chronic stress and more than four times as likely to report physical health symptoms. Among other indicators, those workers were also more likely to say they experienced work–life conflict and felt cynical and negative towards others at work.

Here are some of the ways in which the change and uncertainty of turbulent times might contribute to somebody getting described as difficult at work:

- People who strongly disagree or can't or won't be positively influenced around how you're proposing to change things or how you're dealing with a major uncertainty.

  It's important to find a way to influence how those people feel and, as much as anything, to be influenced by them; to genuinely include their views in your leadership approach.

- People who *internalise* the impacts of that turbulence and, as a result, are likely to suffer themselves.

  Leaders might want to be aware that *any* significant change or uncertainty has the potential to negatively impact people. And that somewhere between one-third and one-half of the people who are affected will internalise it; that is – they will not directly show it.

- People who *externalise* the impacts of that turbulence and who may therefore cause the people around them to suffer as a result.

    In this case, it'll probably be easier to see when that change and uncertainty contribute to somebody being difficult. If not, Chapter 4 has the warning signs to watch out for.

Comfort zone breaches

A major cause that often seems to me to be behind somebody being described as difficult at work is that their comfort zone has been breached in one of two ways. Either they've got way too far outside of it, or they've been outside of it for way too long.

Understanding the comfort zone

Management theorist Alasdair White defined somebody's comfort zone as being that state of mind where:

- things are familiar to them – so they feel at ease; and
- they feel in control – so they have low levels of stress and anxiety.[3]

Growth and optimal performance

Studies have shown that a certain amount of being outside our comfort zone is good for us. Raising the level of challenge that people face, or increasing the number of new, unfamiliar factors puts them into what some researchers have called the 'learning' or 'growth' zones. Only there, it's argued, can people develop and progress. Other researchers have identified a kind of 'optimal performance' zone. In that zone, a certain amount of anxiety and stress actually raises performance at work. But beyond that, performance rapidly declines as stress levels rise.

Being too comfortable isn't necessarily good for people either though. It's been shown that we need some challenge and stress in order to build and maintain the resilience required to handle life and work.

The double-edged sword of stress

Endocrinologist Hans Seyle, using a biochemical analogy, developed the term 'Eustress' from the Greek for 'Good Stress'.[4] Eustress occurs when people have a positive mental response to stress, finding it healthy and fulfilling. It arises when we are slightly pushed out of our comfort zones, but are not overwhelmed by that. Our environment and our goals are familiar enough, but still require us to stretch ourselves. This level of challenge is motivating. It promotes feelings of hope and vitality and provides meaning.

But even this good stress has been shown to be damaging to people's health when it carries on for too long, that is, when it becomes 'chronic'.

Beyond that helpful Eustress is the zone of Distress. In this zone, people are so far out of their comfort zones that the challenges they face cannot be resolved by coping or adapting. Studies indicate that this may lead to anxiety, withdrawal and depressive or aggressive behaviour.

Balancing challenge and support

Research published in the *Journal of Managerial Psychology* suggests that whether or not we have a positive response to something stressful depends on whether it feels controllable or desirable and on when and where it happens (familiar or unfamiliar).[5]

Leaders who want to avoid this possible cause of somebody becoming difficult at work need to be mindful about both the distance and the time for which someone might be outside their comfort zone.

Dimensions of the Matrix of Difficult People

The dimensions of the Matrix of Difficult People are described in detail in Chapter 5. In the context of how those dimensions contribute to somebody being experienced as difficult at work, here's why they matter.

Overused or inappropriate stress strategies

Think of the stress strategies as over-amplified versions of behaviours that have previously been useful for people when they're under pressure.

For example, my own stress strategy typically appears as *Disconnection*. When the going gets tough, it's often been helpful for me to take myself off, have a good think about things and then come back refreshed and with some new ideas to try out.

But it is not always helpful to do that, for example:

- What about situations where disconnection is exactly the *wrong* thing to do? When it might be much better for me to stay around, and become more engaged with things, not less

- What about those times when just a *little* disconnection might have been good but because I'm under pressure my judgement is off and instead of just a little, I do loads of it?

At those times, the stress strategies are like finding myself in a hole and instead of getting out, I just carry on digging it deeper and deeper, more and more furiously!

Inflexible attention focus

We can consider our attention focus as a two-way filter or lens. It selectively influences both what goes *into* our heads – what we notice or pay attention to – and the direction in which it tends to come out again, in the form of what we say and do.

For example, my own default attention focus is on *Systems*.
A systems focus concentrates on the bigger picture of how the different components in a system such as an organisation or business are joined up and how changes to one part might affect the rest.

If I don't think about it, my default systems focus makes me much less interested in the specific *Tasks* that need doing and much less interested in the individual *People* around me. I might not notice what needs doing or who needs my attention. And I might not talk about those issues with other people nor prioritise them when I'm working.

People who are being experienced as difficult at work have often fallen into a very inflexible pattern of attention focus when what is actually needed is the facility to swap focus between Tasks<>Systems<>People as the situation requires.

At those times, an inflexible attention focus is like that old saying, 'If you only have a hammer, everything starts to look like a nail!'

Summary

- -

In this chapter, we've looked at the perfect storm of factors that contribute to someone being experienced as difficult at work. These factors include leadership lapses, turbulent times, breaches in comfort zones, and the dimensions of the Matrix of Difficult People. When these factors overlap, they can create challenging situations for both employees and leaders.

Leadership lapses can make a bad situation worse, with communication, co-ordination and planning, and addressing the 'elephants in the room' being the most significant lapses to look out for. In turbulent times, characterised by change and uncertainty, people are more likely to experience stress and develop negative attitudes, which can contribute to them being experienced as difficult. Comfort zone breaches can also lead to major problems, as being pushed too far or for too long outside one's comfort zone can result in distress and negative behaviour.

The dimensions of the Matrix of Difficult People, as explained in more detail in Chapter 5, revolve around stress strategies and inflexibility in attention focus. Overused or inappropriate stress strategies can exacerbate things, as people may respond in ways that are no longer helpful or not appropriate to the situation. An inflexible attention focus can also lead to problems or make them worse. It may cause people to fixate on those aspects of a situation they're most familiar with, and fail to adapt to the needs of the moment.

Understanding why people become difficult at work can help to find routes for positive change, build emotional intelligence, and adapt to different situations as they arise. By recognising these factors and using the new skills and approaches suggested in Part two of this book, it's possible to create a much more productive and enjoyable way of working together that benefits everyone.

I'm sure there are sometimes other factors involved, but a mix of the four described above generally seems to be present when I've been commissioned to coach someone who has been described as difficult at work. It's natural and useful to ask why this happens, and almost everybody does ask, and with that understanding in place, we can move on.

In the next chapter, we'll take a look at the warning signs that managers and leaders should keep an eye out for, as indicators that someone is being too difficult at work.

Notes

1 Millman, Dan, *Way of the Peaceful Warrior: A Book That Changes Lives*, H J Kramer, 1980.

2 Kotter, John P, 'Accelerate!', *Harvard Business Review*, November 2012.

3 White, Alasdair, 'From comfort zone to performance management', White and MacLean Publishing, October 2009. (First published in Belgium as a PDF/eDoc original in 2009.)

4 Wikipedia Contributors, 'Eustress', Wikipedia. Last modified 7 June 2023; last accessed 22 June 2023.

5 Le Fevre, Mark, Kolt, Gregory S, and Matheny, Jonathan, 'Eustress, distress and their interpretation in primary and secondary occupational stress management interventions: which way first?', *Journal of Managerial Psychology*, Vol. 21 No. 6, 2006, pp. 547–565. Emerald Group Publishing Limited.

chapter 4

Warning signs at work

'Never look down on anybody, unless
you're helping them up.'

Jesse Jackson[1]

Introduction

Identifying the presence of a difficult person at work isn't always straightforward. This chapter presents the critical warning signs to help you recognise a problem and decide when to respond to it.

But how can you spot the warning signs that someone is being difficult at work?

For people who may not have been in this kind of situation before, you might expect the answer to be obvious – if someone who works for or with you is causing a problem, surely you'd already know?

The answer to that question seems to be *'Yes, but . . . '*.

Yes, most managers and colleagues would already have noticed at least a few signs that something wasn't quite right. But, most people are also extremely reluctant to risk making a bad situation worse.

They might not want to make a big fuss because at the beginning you can't tell just how difficult someone could get. They're also often reluctant to believe the evidence or to trust their intuition that something is up, preferring to give people the benefit of the doubt. Moreover, people often don't act until they're forced to by a crisis of some kind, because it's not always easy to know just what you *can* do to help.

Leadership can also be quite a distant practice in today's organisations. Remote working, wide spans of control and the sheer pace of things can mean that a leader's immediate experience of someone who has become difficult may be quite limited.

Even when they have decided to act, as they are commissioning me, leaders will often say: *'Well, I wouldn't describe them as a difficult person exactly, but . . . '*. They recognise that something is up, but are understandably reluctant to start labelling a colleague as 'difficult'.

Difficult people themselves also find it hard to ask for help. It can feel risky to expose ourselves in that situation. It's hard to know what kind of reaction we might get if we tell colleagues that we're struggling and people are understandably concerned that it might be career-limiting. And it's not always obvious that there is a good way to turn the situation around. Again, people are unlikely to act until the pain of *not* doing something becomes worse than the pain of trying to change things.

Use this chapter to help understand what signs you might be missing or to help confirm something that your intuition might already have been telling you.

Bruised, blocked or burnt out

Your own interactions with one specific person are leaving you feeling the pain.

Is there one specific person at work who often leaves you feeling particularly bruised by your interactions? Or who seems to block your attempts to get things done? Or who takes up so much of your time and effort that you're often tired and burnt out from trying?

Here's what it will probably feel like if you're the manager or colleague of someone who seems difficult in this way.

Bruised

You may notice that every encounter with this person leaves you feeling bruised. It wasn't quite a boxing match, but it did feel a bit like a fight, as if you always have to stand your ground with them. There's little subtlety, and almost every point they make has the force of a punch behind it. Or perhaps you're often left feeling that you've somehow been judged by them, getting a sense that you're not living up to their exacting standards. Even when you think you're in agreement, or at least operating from the same agenda, interacting with this person is bruising.

Blocked

What about the person who has a really good reason why every idea, initiative and objective you suggest just can't happen? Who blocks the progress you and your colleagues would like to see? There's always something else that needs to be done first, or a detail you're overlooking, a knock-on impact you've discounted, a rule you'd fall foul of. Your experience with this kind of person is likely to have you feeling blocked at every turn.

Burnt out

Some people have levels of drive and energy that are way in excess of others. Their commitment often inspires great loyalty but being around them, managing them, or just trying to keep up with them can sometimes come at a cost. One client's boss described him as being: 'Like a supernova in a box. And I'm worried about the state of the box!' Experiencing this type of person in the wrong circumstances can leave you and others feeling exhausted or even burnt out.

Consistently feeling bruised, blocked or burnt out by someone is a useful sign that they might have fallen into the trap of being difficult at work – and could use some support.

A great escape

Junior staff, colleagues and even customers are leaving the business in big numbers.

The impact of a difficult person on staff turnover

Often the first clear sign that there's a difficult person somewhere in your business is a great escape – a mass outbreak of other people leaving. People you'd invested time and money in recruiting and developing. And who may well be headed into the open arms of your competitors.

A client told me what was happening at their business. As a result of one or two people, this professional services firm had found itself losing junior partners at a slow but worrying rate. In our first briefing session, they explained that the cost to the firm of losing just one junior partner could be as much as £100k, just in the loss of fees they'd suffer before that person could be replaced. This excludes the costs of actually replacing that person, which some studies put at up to twice the annual salary for a highly educated executive position.

If it's professional staff who are leaving and they are actually taking their own portfolio of clients with them as they go, then of course the whole situation gets even more alarming for the business concerned.

The role of managers in employee retention

It's a well-known saying that employees join companies but leave managers.

A Gallup poll of more than 1 million workers in the USA in 2008 concluded that the number one reason people leave their jobs is because of a bad boss or immediate supervisor. They found that 75 per cent of workers who voluntarily left their jobs did so because of their bosses.[2]

If you're not already aware of what's going on, exit interviews could help by providing an opportunity for owners and senior leaders to investigate those reasons personally.

Exit interviews and organisational response

However, research by the *Harvard Business Review* suggests that less than one-third of exit interviews actually result in a change of policy or in an intervention of some kind.[3] This implies that in many instances companies know what is going on, but don't act. Many organisations simply don't know what kind of effective intervention might be possible in order to deal with a difficult person – and are frozen into inaction.

To be on the safe side if a great escape is happening in your organisation, at least consider it as a warning sign that something is not right – and investigate further.

On shaky ground

An uneasy feeling that gaps will open up or that critical issues won't be addressed.

Clients sometimes describe this 'shaky ground' experience, just before they discover that someone is being difficult at work. It's a sense of unknown unreliability. They go to lean on something, but it's not there. They think they're on solid ground, but then they realise that it's wobbly, or feel like it might open up beneath their feet. Here's what to look out for.

Lack of confidence

The kids in my family played rugby and every now and then one of them would find themselves underneath a high ball, getting ready to catch it. When you're a teenager and the team is relying on you and everybody's watching, it's a big deal to be under a high ball like that. You can see who is worried about catching the ball. You can see them thinking: *'I mustn't drop it.'*

This is the phenomenon of hyper-focus which I've written more about in the relevant chapters of Part two. It's the self-fulfilling part of this phenomenon which causes problems at work. If people think they're going to drop the ball, they're more likely to do so. Is part of your shaky ground, that sense of unknown unreliability, being caused by a difficult person lacking in confidence?

Stress-driven disappearances

You're likely to notice this more as a kind of absence. You go to rely on something, but discover it hasn't been done. You think progress is being made and then, when it's almost too late, you uncover a whole load of unresolved problems.

One of my commissioning clients likened it to those sinkholes that occasionally open up under a busy road. Everything looked fine until whatever was undermining things finally caused the surface to give way.

The Disconnection and Avoidance stress strategies in my matrix are what happens to individual difficult people who might be contributing to your sense of unease. Are these the gaps that you're worried might be about to open up in your organisation's capabilities?

The cost – if things don't come to light in time

Project Management experts 4PM estimated in 2015 that most organisations have project failure rates of around 70 per cent – where project success is defined as producing the planned deliverables, within the budget, on time, and allowing for approved changes.[4] The IT and business services giant IBM says that just 40 per cent of their *own* projects meet their three key goals around schedule, budget and quality.[5]

The Project Management Institute's research also shows that a total of 51 per cent of project failures are caused by a combination of poor communication, lack of communication by senior management, and employee resistance.[6] And these are certainly the kind of issues we're considering.

Trust your instincts and act earlier if you get that sense of shaky ground beneath your feet. It may be that there is someone in difficulty behind it.

Toxic culture

No matter how hard you try, there's a whole unit delivering almost nothing positive.

The impact of toxic leaders

Peter Drucker famously said that 'Culture eats strategy for breakfast.'[7] This can come disastrously true when someone is being difficult in a way that infects the culture of a whole business department or subsidiary.

It's been described to me as a kind of 'toxic wasteland', where it's almost impossible to achieve anything worthwhile and even surviving can become a real challenge.

Survival tactics in a toxic environment

When a toxic wasteland does take hold, it's often because the board has appointed a potentially difficult person to tackle a big challenge – the kind of person who believes that you can't make an omelette without breaking eggs. If that person then struggles under the pressure to deliver and isn't supported properly, then the people around them may start to adopt survival tactics. Instead of focusing on getting the job done and having good working relationships, they're likely to start doing whatever it takes to not become a victim themselves, including collaborating with the toxic way of doing things.

I'm not talking here about those situations where something tough needs doing regardless of a few complaints about the effort. A toxic situation is where the overall culture is acting directly *against* achieving what's actually needed. No matter how many eggs get broken, no wholesome omelette is getting cooked there!

Engaged employees and organisational success

The Centre for Business Venturing has been running an annual survey for over ten years now.[8] The survey looks at the benefits of having 'engaged employees', which they describe as the extent to which '. . . employees are committed to the success of the organisation they work for'. The survey shows that organisations with engaged employees have:

- Sixty-five per cent greater share-price increase
- Twenty-six per cent less employee turnover
- One hundred per cent more unsolicited employment applications
- Twenty per cent less absenteeism
- Fifteen per cent greater employee productivity
- Up to thirty per cent greater customer satisfaction levels.

Those are some fairly big benefits from getting your culture right, and it's easy to see which metrics would be adversely affected when the culture is wrong.

If you notice signs that the culture might have become toxic, it's worth looking into whether a difficult person might be at the heart of it.

Summary

- -

It's fairly common and understandable for people to overlook the evidence or to set aside their intuition that someone might have become difficult at work. First, it's not always easy to tell if this might be happening. Second, we're naturally inclined to think the best of people and to give them the benefit of the doubt.

And third, without a process like the one in this book, it isn't always possible to see what positive steps we *can* take to do something about it. So it's overlooked, until things get to the point where they really start to cause problems and can't be left any longer and we're forced to take possibly drastic action.

The four warning signs described in this chapter can help to spot when this might be the case. We can identify feelings of being bruised, blocked or burnt out by someone. We can see the signs that there's a great escape – an exodus of other people leaving, possibly because of one difficult person. We can notice how the ground around us somehow seems shaky, when things have become unreliable. And we can test for a toxic culture: those occasions when the reactions of a difficult person might have created an atmosphere where nothing can flourish.

Identifying those warning signs helps to clear the way for managers, leaders and colleagues to start the process of changing things for the better. And to do so earlier, before anything reaches a crisis point.

The next chapter shows how the two related dimensions of my matrix can combine under the wrong circumstances to end up with a difficult person at work.

Notes

1 Jackson, Jesse (n.d.), as cited in 'Jesse Jackson quotes'. BrainyQuote. Last accessed 22 June 2023.

2 Robison, Jennifer, 'Turning around employee turnover.' *Gallup Business Journal*. 8 May 2008. Last accessed 22 June 2023.

3 Holtom, Brooks C, and Everett Spain, 'Making exit interviews count', *Harvard Business Review*, April 2016. Last accessed 22 June 2023.

4 4PM.com (2019), as cited in 'Most projects fail to deliver', Bartley Joseph, LinkedIn Pulse. Published 5 March 2019. Last accessed 22 June 2023.

5 Andriole, Steve, 'Why no one can manage projects, especially technology projects', Forbes, 1 December 2020. Last accessed 22 June 2023.

6 Project Management Institute, Inc., 'The high cost of low performance: the essential role of communications', PMI, May 2013.

7 Drucker, Peter (n.d.), as cited in 'Culture eats strategy for breakfast – The Management Centre', The Management Centre. Last accessed 22 June 2023.

8 Pleiter, Shelley, 'Engaging employees', Smith Business Insight, Smith School of Business at Queen's University, in association with The Queen's Centre for Business Venturing, Winter 2014.

chapter 5

The Matrix of Difficult People at Work

'Seek first to understand.'

Stephen Covey[1]

Introduction

The Matrix of Difficult People introduced in this chapter is a way of understanding what's going on when someone seems too difficult at work, with a view to doing something about it.

People react in different ways when they're under pressure, and they have different priorities for how they see and respond to the world around them. That's why the same kind of situations can produce quite different patterns in the ways that people are experienced as difficult. With the matrix and the quick quiz in Chapter 6, we can identify those underlying patterns and use the rest of this book to quickly target any actions we want to take.

Of course, discovering types of people doesn't tell us *everything* about a specific person. Nor does it totally define everybody who might resemble that type. The usefulness of a tool like the matrix is not to pigeonhole people, but to support understanding and investigation. Then we can help people to generate more behavioural choices and more flexibility of approach in a way that works for everybody.

The two related dimensions that combine to produce the matrix are *attention focus* and *stress strategy,* shown in the Matrix of Difficult People here and covered in the rest of this chapter.

		Attention Focus		
		Tasks	Systems	People
Stress Strategy	Disconnection	1. Scary Specialist	2. Dark Strategist	3. Martyr
	Excess	4. Driving Force	5. Revolutionary	6. Empire Builder
	Avoidance	7. Worrier	8. Rock	9. People Pleaser

The Matrix of Difficult People

Attention Focus

A set of traits which, if applied inflexibly and in combination with a stress strategy, tend to lead to people being experienced as difficult.

An attention focus trait is a product of someone's prevailing preferences for how they:

- Receive and process different kinds of information and experiences; and

- Relate to the other people and things around them.

One way to think of attention focus is as a two-way filter, selectively influencing both what goes *into* our heads and the direction in which it tends to come *out* again in what we say and do.

Unlike the stress strategies, there is nothing intrinsically wrong with any of the attention focus traits themselves. Each of them is a potentially useful way of operating at work, with benefits and downsides of their own.

There are three attention focus traits:

Task focus

Focus is on discrete tasks or projects that have tangible outcomes.

This person will give the most consideration to what needs to be done, filtering out other issues from their thoughts and behaviours. They'll assess progress and set priorities around tasks with tangible outcomes both in their own work and with their team.

Systems focus

Focus is on the interconnectedness and meshing together of different systems and processes.

This person will give the most consideration to how (or if) things join up, tending to filter out specific tasks or individual people's feelings from their thoughts and actions. They'll be concerned with the bigger picture and with how changes to one component affect the rest of the system.

People focus

The focus is on people and the thoughts, feelings and social status they hold.

This person will give the most consideration to the people in their organisation, to their needs, opinions and influence. They will assess and prioritise work projects and be concerned with the operating environment and corporate agenda in terms of the impact they have on people.

Stress Strategy

The ways in which people sometimes apply distorted versions of their strengths to try and deal with challenging circumstances.

Things can often get tricky at work when people are:

- Operating outside of their comfort zones – either too far or for too long
- Facing obstacles that they find too difficult or scary; or
- Lacking the guidance of really effective leadership.

For any of us in that kind of situation, it can be a stretch. We might find it hard to keep our motivation and balance going. We might struggle to behave consistently and effectively or to find the right mix of empathy and challenge for others.

Now imagine someone in that kind of situation who hasn't learned how to *vary* their approach to suit such testing circumstances. What my coaching work reveals is that someone in that position is quite likely to adopt a behavioural strategy based on their *existing* strengths – but get that strategy wrong.

Initially, a behavioural strategy based on existing strengths makes sense – under pressure stick to doing things in the way that worked before.

The trouble occurs when the old way doesn't work any longer, either because:

- Circumstances have changed and now require a different approach; or
- Pressure causes people to adopt over-amplified, grossly distorted versions of what have previously been their strengths.

I call those distorted versions of existing strengths the stress strategies and there are three of them:

Disconnection

When a healthy sense of separateness goes wrong.

Setting high standards for our own areas, keeping space around important work so that it's got room to develop and having well-defined boundaries are normally a healthy and useful part of what it takes to succeed at work.

Disconnection occurs when you have too much of that separation at the wrong times. When, under pressure, people tend to really separate themselves from those who are outside their circle of trust and respect.

Excess

When energy and ambition get in the way.

Inspiring change, disrupting outdated approaches and delivering demanding assignments are normally highly valued qualities.

Excess occurs when someone's *only* response to challenging circumstances is to do more of those things at the wrong times. When, under pressure, people tend to excessively ramp up the level of energy/pressure or scope of ambition that they bring to bear.

Avoidance

When safety is self-defeating.

Ensuring that things are done properly, creating harmony and steering clear of criticism are important parts of what usually makes organisations run smoothly.

Avoidance occurs when that safe approach becomes counterproductive, at that time creating more problems than it solves. When, under pressure, people try too hard to avoid errors, conflict, change or rejection.

In each case, problems can arise at work when the most appropriate focus for the situation is not the one that someone unconsciously tends to adopt. If they can't smoothly and authentically shift their focus to match the people and circumstances around them, things start to get tricky. And if you combine an inflexible attention focus with an out-of-control stress strategy – that's when people become difficult!

My quick quiz in the next chapter will help you identify which type of difficult person you might be dealing with.

Note

1 Covey, Stephen R, *The 7 Habits of Highly Effective People: Powerful Lessons in Personal Change*, New York: Simon & Schuster, 1989.

chapter 6

Quick quiz to identify types

'Discovery consists of looking at the same thing as everyone else and thinking something different.'

Albert Szent-Gyorgyi[1]

Introduction

The quick quiz in this chapter will identify which type of difficult person you might be dealing with.

One of the reasons many difficult situations at work continue to fester or even get worse over time is that it's sometimes hard to know what to do about them. Or even whether there *is* anything that can be done without making more of a mess of things. This quick quiz, and the way it relates the behaviours you've experienced to the dimensions of my matrix, provides a pragmatic and tailored way forwards so that you can start to make a difference.

Follow the instructions below to take the quick quiz and then compare your answers to the table at the end of this chapter.

Instructions

Step 1: Visualise the difficult person

- Think about the person in question.
- Create a mental image of them.

Step 2: Recall your experiences

- Remember your interactions with this person.
- Consider how they made you feel.

Step 3: Gather additional information

- Think about any other details you know about their behaviour at work.

Step 4: Review the descriptions

- There are two groups of descriptions, each with three options: Group One (A, B, C) and Group Two (I, II, III).
- Read each option in both groups.

Step 5: Choose the best match

- For each group, pick the option that best describes the difficult person.
- Don't worry if you don't agree with every point; focus on the overall description.

Step 6: Narrow down your choices (optional)

- If you're unsure, eliminate the least-fitting options in each group and select the remaining one.

Step 7: Use your intuition

- Trust your gut feeling when making a choice.
- You can always revisit the quiz later if needed.

Step 8: Final selection

- Your final selection will be a combination of one capital letter (from Group One) and one Roman numeral (from Group Two).

Step 9: Begin your selection

- Start by reviewing the options in Group One.

Group one

Select one option from Group one – A, B or C.

A

This person's focus is typically at the level of discrete tasks or projects that have tangible outcomes. They want to get things done.

You may recognise them because they talk about what needs doing next, or what is the most pressing objective, or about a measurable result that was just achieved.

You may notice they become impatient, distracted or even uncomprehending if you question them about the needs and preferences of specific people around them. Similarly, they may be unlikely to share (or even recognise) many of their own emotions, apart from a sense of intolerance towards others.

They may prefer not to lead or take part in activities which require wide-ranging co-operation between departments. They prefer to take approaches that they know have previously worked for them or for others.

B

This person's focus is typically at the level of systems, at the interconnectedness and necessary meshing-together of different systems and processes. They are interested in 'how'; whether it's how to create change or how to optimise an approach or method.

You may recognise them talking about chains of consequences: 'If you change that, it will affect this,' or 'If we want to do X, then first we have to do Y.'

You may notice they become frustrated (and frustrating) if the people and workflows around them do not take such interdependencies into account or fail to grasp the big picture of how things need to align together.

They are likely to act with more autonomy than they should and either do what they think needs doing anyway or complain about doing what they believe to be inadequate.

C

This person's focus is typically on the level of people and the thoughts, feelings and social status that they hold. They are interested in both 'who' – which specific individuals or which groups of people are involved, as well as 'why' – why does somebody feel that way, and why should a certain task be important to people?

You may recognise that they frequently name specific individuals or groups when talking about their work.

You may notice they become highly concerned about things that might have an adverse impact on relationships at work. Similarly, they prefer colleagues and team members with whom they can establish high levels of rapport and loyalty.

They are likely to organise their work around people, either in the way that they build teams and design workflows or as a goal in itself.

Group two

Next, select one option from Group Two – I, II or III.

I

This person has a tendency to 'circle the wagons', putting up a barrier around themselves or what they perceive to be their domain. It often feels like they're disconnected from you or other parts of the organisation.

They might keep their team or department separate as well. You may notice that they try to 'protect' their team members, perhaps by restricting access to them or by not cascading down to them messages or requests from the wider organisation.

It can seem hard to truly win this person's trust or to completely gain their respect. You and other people may often feel judged or be made to feel inadequate by them. They may sabotage any attempts to control their domain – or sabotage attempts to change things which might indirectly impact their own degree of control.

II

This person has a tendency to go all in or head on, bringing large amounts of energy and pressure to bear all over the place. It often seems like their response to everything is to ramp up the effort or to expand their scope.

You may notice that their team members or the people around them get burnt out: overloaded by the range and complexity of what's being attempted, dropping by the wayside because of the pace, or being unable to tackle yet another difficult task head on.

Your interactions with them may often make you feel both weary and wary. Weary because their energy levels or the challenge they bring to things are tiring. And wary because you feel the need to constantly be reining them in, alert to the risk of them crossing the wrong boundary or upsetting the wrong people.

III

This person has a tendency to duck conflicts, avoid changes and worry excessively about what could go wrong. You may notice your interactions with them are characterised by a kind of 'absence'; as if there was a gap in your defences. Or like trying to work with one hand tied behind your back.

Even though you might like them, it often feels as if they're unreliable – failing to address tricky issues that you'd agreed on, putting roadblocks in the way of change you'd asked them to deliver, or dropping the ball in crucial moments.

They may cause team members and colleagues to be both uncomfortable – waiting for something bad to happen – and undisciplined – taking advantage of the situation. You may need to pay close attention to spot it, but what this person most wants to feel is 'safe'.

Quick quiz answers and the different types

The matrix below shows the answers to your quick quiz.

For example, if you selected option 'C' from Group one and option 'II' from Group two, you've identified the Empire Builder.

		Group one		
		A	**B**	**C**
Group two	I	1. Scary Specialist	2. Dark Strategist	3. Martyr
	II	4. Driving Force	5. Revolutionary	6. Empire Builder
	III	7. Worrier	8. Rock	9. People Pleaser

Answers to quick quiz

You can confirm your results using the outline descriptions of each type in the next chapter, then move straight on to the flowchart and dynamic principles to get into action.

Note

1 Szent-Gyorgyi, Albert (n.d.), as cited in 'Discovery consists of seeing what everybody has seen and thinking what nobody has thought', Book Browse. Last accessed 22 June 2023.

chapter 7

Summary of types

'Just because I can't control
the sea doesn't mean I can't learn
how to swim in it.'

Rami Shapiro[1]

This chapter sets out a short summary of each of the nine types for quick reference. More detailed descriptions and suggestions for dealing with them are covered in Part two of this book.

1. The Scary Specialist

The Scary Specialist is usually an expert in their field, with a deep and valuable understanding of a particular area.

Key characteristics: This person is extremely competent and results-driven and sets a very high standard for their work.

Why others can find them difficult: Issues at work can arise from their non-negotiable demands that other people be just as high-performing as they are. And that any resources, processes and support areas that are outside of their domain but which affect or contribute to its functioning are perfect.

2. The Dark Strategist

The Dark Strategist is usually someone who likes having a grand plan and will work behind the scenes to perfect it.

Key characteristics: They are insightful and ambitious, driven to figure out all that's required to achieve a key goal or to realise a step-change in the business.

Why others can find them difficult: Issues at work can arise when they've tried to move people and partner organisations around without question or autonomy, treating others like chess pieces as they try to deliver their plan.

3. The Martyr

The Martyr is usually a highly principled person, with a strong sense of justice and a clear belief that things should be improved for the betterment of all.

Key characteristics: This person has an extremely high work ethic and a profound care for others. They often inspire deep loyalty in their followers.

Why others can find them difficult: Issues at work can arise from their refusal to compromise for an imperfect solution, from the judgements they make about others whom they see as less principled, and from the self-sacrifice and inability to progress that this can lead to.

4. The Driving Force

The Driving Force is usually a very resourceful, decisive and can-do person. They believe in their ability to overcome obstacles and, if necessary, to learn how to do so as they go.

Key characteristics: This person is likely to be a leader, perhaps heading up a large department or running a small independent consultancy. They love to rise to a challenge.

Why others can find them difficult: Issues at work tend to arise because of their low tolerance for colleagues who won't also meet every challenge head on; when they become impatient with the 'timid' corporate agenda; and when they have bitten off more than they can chew and need to retrench rapidly.

5. The Revolutionary

The Revolutionary is usually a self-starting, enthusiastic person who is great at finding out about new ideas and different approaches.

Key characteristics: This person readily embraces change and will push for fast and wide-ranging transformation regardless of its wider implications.

Why others can find them difficult: Issues at work can arise from their desire to change everything as far and as fast as possible, often acting without consensus or regard for fallout.

6. The Empire Builder

The Empire Builder is usually a charismatic and visionary person with a powerful ability to recruit people to their cause.

Key characteristics: They have a strong self-belief, rely on their supporters to handle the details and often come to the fore as leaders in times of uncertainty or challenge.

Why others can find them difficult: Issues at work can arise from their tendency to sweep up more and more control, regardless of whether that is the best thing to do overall, from their intolerance of criticism, and from their disregard for inconvenient complications.

7. The Worrier

The Worrier is usually a very conscientious and responsible person who takes their job seriously.

Key characteristics: They want to be helpful and to add value without needing to be in the limelight. They often have a good sense of right and wrong and are typically very detail-focused.

Why others can find them difficult: Issues at work can arise from a focus on what might go wrong and a struggle to see the bigger picture. These can lead to micromanaging, difficulties with influencing, and sensitivity around protecting 'their' turf.

8. The Rock

The Rock is usually a highly responsible and committed person, with a deep sense of loyalty to the organisation.

Key characteristics: They'll be quietly and steadily doing whatever it takes to ensure that important systems and processes are running properly.

Why others can find them difficult: Issues at work can arise because of their silent and immovable refusal to do anything that might expose the business to risk, especially if they believe that someone hasn't understood the knock-on consequences of a course of action.

9. The People Pleaser

The People Pleaser is usually a warm self-effacing person who has built up a real depth of experience and a wide network of trusted and trusting connections.

Key characteristics: They value harmony and teamwork, and want their area to do well. They like to keep people onboard so they can make incremental improvements.

Why others can find them difficult: Issues at work can arise when they are avoiding conflicts, overlooking big changes that might rock the boat, or not actively contributing to the wider agenda, so that risks are undeclared and opportunities missed.

The next chapter offers my three Dynamic Principles: the guidelines and mindset that have been most helpful in setting out to deal with someone who is being difficult at work, in a balanced and effective way.

Note

1 Shapiro, Rami (n.d.), as cited in 'Quotes by Rami M. Shapiro', Goodreads. Last accessed 22 June 2023.

chapter 8

Three dynamic principles to fine-tune your mindset

'An army of principles can penetrate where an army of soldiers cannot.'

Thomas Paine[1]

Introduction

In this chapter, you'll discover the three principles likely to assist most in shaping your strategy for dealing with difficult people. They're rooted in the guiding principles I've found most useful and effective in my own coaching work.

I've called them 'Dynamic principles' because there's a certain amount of energy or tension to be balanced, whether it is that understanding needs to be a two-way street, as in positive intention vs. actual impact. Or that seemingly opposite qualities such as fierce kindness can provide a deeper and more fruitful way of operating. Or that there's often an interdependence, such as empowered agency, that needs to be actively maintained.

Positive Intention vs. Actual Impact

Workplace behaviour can sometimes be hard to comprehend or accept. This is especially so when people say or do things that feel hurtful, critical, dismissive or uncaring, or seem deliberately hostile or aimed at generating conflict.

Understanding positive intention

It's useful to understand that, from their perspective, the result they're trying to get is almost always a positive one.

Whether they're trying to deal with something they find challenging, wanting to push forwards an issue they feel is important, aiming to protect the team, or simply struggling to cope. An intention might seem negative on the surface, but it can still be positive if we consider the broader context and the person's underlying motivation.

Benefits and downsides of positive-intention-seeking

Adopting the viewpoint that people at work are actually trying to contribute positively to organisational success is helpful, as it:

- Cultivates empathy and eases interactions – adopting this viewpoint helps manage challenging situations by fostering understanding and clear communication

- Boosts relationships and reduces conflicts – it improves workplace relationships and facilitates collaboration, which then also leads to better conflict resolution.

Unbalanced positive-intention-seeking, however, has downsides, particularly when dealing with a genuinely difficult person. It can lead to:

- Overlooking or downplaying problematic behaviour, where issues are allowed to persist or even escalate

- Putting too much of the responsibility to understand and adjust onto others, as other people are always expected to accommodate a difficult person's actions without addressing the root causes

- Inadvertently enabling toxic or manipulative behaviour, which then harms relationships and performance at work.

Balancing positive intention with actual impact

On its own positive intention is an extremely useful viewpoint, but it isn't always enough to create constructive change. It needs to be dynamically balanced with an emphasis on the impact of a person's behaviour. The key is to consider the following. As a result of what someone said or did:

- What changed?
- On the whole, was it a positive outcome?
- How were people feeling afterwards?

We need to understand and reveal positive intention – the underlying positive motivation and the outcome that someone was aiming for – and then compare that with the outcome that was achieved, their actions' real impact.

Fierce Kindness

People at work have different ways of understanding, behaving and communicating, even in identical situations to others. Almost inevitably this can lead to misunderstandings and clashes, which are made worse when someone is under enough pressure and/or being difficult.

Fierce kindness is the second principle that can really help to resolve things for the better.

Fierce

The 'fierce' component encourages you to tackle difficult situations head on. It involves:

- **Assertive communication:** clearly and respectfully stating your thoughts, feelings and needs
- **Boundary-setting:** establishing and maintaining limits to protect your well-being and productivity. There are different types of boundaries that need to be covered, and I've set out each in the relevant sections of Part two.

Kindness

On the other hand, the 'kindness' aspect of fierce kindness focuses on understanding and empathy. It involves:

- **Listening properly:** with full attention, to understand others' perspectives

- **Demonstrating empathy:** acknowledging and validating other people's feelings
- **Offering support:** encouraging people, particularly towards collaboration and mutual problem-solving.

Potential downsides of each alone

As with my other principles, what's needed here is a dynamic combination of both approaches. If we don't actively work towards that balance then:

- Fierce alone can be (or be perceived as) confrontational, possibly leading to increased tension and more misunderstandings
- Kindness alone may result in excessive leniency, allowing detrimental behaviour to persist and negatively affect the work environment. Or in unprotected boundaries, magnifying the negative impacts.

Dynamically balanced fierce kindness

Fierce and kind elements, when actively used together, create a balanced approach, which is both assertive and compassionate. This balance is essential because:

- The combination of assertiveness and empathy means you can take practical steps to address the issue while still considering the feelings and perspectives of the person involved
- It helps to build an environment of trust and open, honest communication. Then you can have difficult conversations without someone being afraid of retaliation or of being alienated
- It promotes collaborative problem-solving, as you're encouraging skills that let everybody feel heard and respected, and which lead to more effective and sustainable solutions.

Empowered Agency

There's also a more strategic viewpoint to consider. This is the principle of empowered agency, which helps to provide a slightly higher perspective for navigating challenging situations.

Empowerment

Empowerment is the process of providing individuals or teams with the necessary authority, resources and support to make decisions, take responsibility and achieve their goals. It involves fostering a culture of trust, open communication and collaboration.

Agency

Agency refers to an individual's own capacity to act independently, make choices and exert control, rather than being solely subject to external forces. This encompasses people grasping opportunities to direct their own tasks, contribute to decision-making, ask for support and express their ideas. Agency is not a fixed trait, but more a skill that can be developed.

Why they don't work alone

If agency is the inherent ability to take control and make choices, then empowerment is the external support and environment that allows people to exercise their agency properly at work.

Here's what happens if they're not balanced with each other:

- **Empowerment without agency** – for example, a team leader delegates tasks and provides resources to their team members (*empowerment*) but keeps them out of the decisions about what needs doing (*agency*). As a result, they actually feel *disempowered* and lack ownership, motivation and accountability.

- **Agency without empowerment** – for example, someone is great at developing new ideas to improve a product (*agency*) but isn't allowed to make decisions about it or to access resources (*empowerment*). They become frustrated and disengage.

The synergistic balance

Dealing with difficult people at work can be a daunting task, but the empowered agency principle offers a powerful tool for addressing these challenges.

By synergistically combining agency and empowerment, we can create an environment that is useful for managing difficult people at work for several reasons:

- **Responsibility** – people are encouraged to take responsibility for what they say and do, enabling more constructive discussions and better conflict handling.

- **Communication** – people are able to express their concerns and opinions while feeling supported by their leaders, helping to identify and solve potential issues before they get worse.

- **Empathy** – when people feel both empowered and have agency, they are more likely to empathise with others and understand different perspectives, leading to improved workplace relationships.

The next chapter sets out a big-picture view of what's involved in dealing with a difficult person at work in the form of a flowchart.

Note

1 Thomas Paine – pamphlet, 'Agrarian justice', as cited by U.S. Social Security Administration, Office of Policy, Office of Research, Evaluation, and Statistics. Last accessed 22 June 2023.

chapter 9

Visual flowchart

'Art, like morality, consists of drawing
the line somewhere.'

G.K. Chesterton[1]

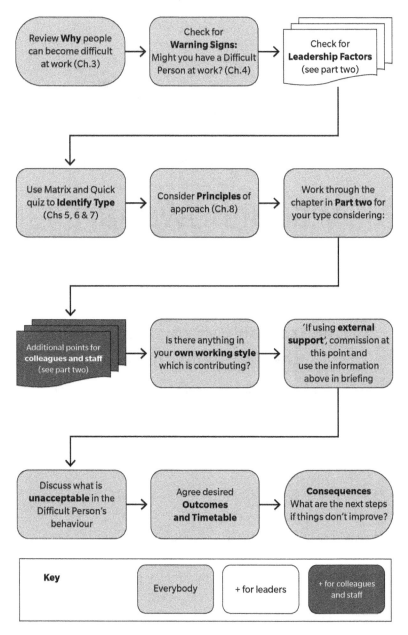

Figure 1 Flowchart for dealing with difficult people – Part one

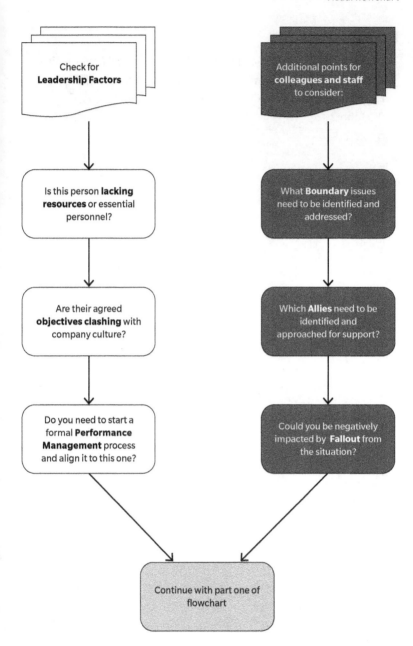

Figure 2 Flowchart for dealing with difficult people – Part two

Note

1 Chesterton, G.K., 'Our note book', *The Illustrated London News*, 5 May 1928, as cited in 'Art, like morality, consists of drawing the line somewhere – Quote Investigator'. Last accessed 22 June 2023.

part 2

chapter 10

Type 1 – The Scary Specialist

'Be so good they can't ignore you.'

Steve Martin[1]

In a nutshell

The Scary Specialist is usually an expert in their field, with a deep and valuable understanding of a particular area.

Key characteristics: This person is extremely competent and results-driven and sets a very high standard for their work.

Why others can find them difficult: Issues at work can arise from their non-negotiable demands that other people be just as high-performing as they are. And that any resources, processes and support areas that are outside of their domain but which affect or contribute to its functioning are perfect.

Example

Charlotte is highly qualified in her field and over the years has built a strong reputation for quickly delivering only the best results. She always asks a lot of her team and expects the people around her to be as committed and competent as she is. She prefers it when the other parts of the organisation are running efficiently and faultlessly, leaving her and her team alone to get on with things.

At their best

They are a valued member of the business or organisation, delivering important high-quality results again and again. As a leader, they will work hard to create the conditions for similarly committed and driven people to really shine. Working alongside them, when things are going well (and if you can take the pace), can be a tremendously thrilling and satisfying experience. They can often be the powerhouse of a business or other organisation, generating profits, providing important services and setting the pace for success.

When do things get difficult?

Above all, the Scary Specialist values competence, drive and independence – and the level of performance that these qualities can deliver.

When they are leading or are part of a team where all these qualities are present then things can be great. Change one of these components – threaten their independence, replace a high-performing team member with somebody who's not quite up to it, or otherwise affect their ability to deliver quality and deliver it fast – and you can be in big trouble no matter what your intention was.

In those circumstances, the Scary Specialist is likely to become extremely challenging, obstructive and critical. They may become directly critical in circumstances when they feel safe to brutally say what they think. Or indirectly critical, in the form of sniping and complaining when it concerns people who also have power in the organisation.

Their place in the Matrix of Difficult People

	T	S	P
D	😐	💥	😇
E	😠	🙂	😎
A	😬	😑	😳

Attention Focus

Task focused – the Scary Specialist's primary focus, and the lens through which they assess things, is on discrete tasks or projects that have tangible outcomes.

Stress Strategy

Disconnection – under pressure, the Scary Specialist will tend to separate themselves or their domain, disconnecting from those who are outside their safe circle of trust, respect and/or control.

How to spot a Scary Specialist

Collateral damage

You might notice other people complaining of their interactions with the Scary Specialist, how they felt threatened, belittled or locked out. You may see new recruits leaving almost as quickly as they arrived. You might also experience a sudden and sustained uptick in rates of turnover, as several long-standing people decide to quit rather than tolerate a difficult person situation.

Tiptoeing around their threats or demands

You might notice yourself or colleagues tiptoeing around the Scary Specialist, postponing tricky discussions or decisions, or feeling like you're walking on eggshells, where one wrong move could set things off badly.

They may block key strategic changes if they perceive a threat to 'their' domain. They are likely to make demands for colleagues or managers to fix processes, systems or support functions that they perceive as not being up to scratch. They may adopt bullying behaviour towards weaker, under-performing colleagues or members of their team with the unstated (perhaps even unconscious) aim of forcing them out.

The drawbridge is up

The Disconnection response is part of the Scary Specialist's strategy for dealing with stressful situations and with their need to maintain a high level of output and quality. They will turn inwards, jealously guarding the area over which they have control and/or responsibility. You may notice that disconnection itself, or you might first become aware of an absence of their participation in anything other than their domain. It's a pulling-up of the drawbridge or a circling of the wagons, so that only their domain matters, together with a very definite 'keep out' attitude towards anybody or anything that might trespass on that domain.

Tips for leaders of a Scary Specialist

When things are going well, leading a Scary Specialist is easy.

Their commitment to competence and to delivering high levels of quality outputs will make them a valued and inspirational member of your business, raising the bar on what you do and how well you do it. They will be constantly looking for improvements, alert to feedback from clients, customers or service users and highly attuned to the kind of advantageous nuance of approach that only someone with deep knowledge or experience can spot.

Leaders often say that their Scary Specialist can be relied on to deliver. Which paradoxically can be a problem, if leaders have got used to being a little too hands off.

If the situation has reached the point where as a leader you feel you do need to intervene, you'll want to consider:

- Just how valuable is this Scary Specialist, compared to the damage they might be causing? Would it be too great a risk, to lose them altogether?

- Is your own leadership style contributing? For example, leaders who also have a task focus may tend to ignore the negative impacts that the Scary Specialist can sometimes have on people and systems.

- What's your scope for taking action? For example, Scary Specialists can sometimes wield a great deal of power in their organisations and leaders may need to build consensus with other colleagues before they can effectively intervene.

Once (or if) you've decided that it is time to take action, here are my three main strategies for leading a Scary Specialist who is being unacceptably difficult.

Rearrange things around them

Perhaps your Scary Specialist is so crucial to your business that it's worth putting significant effort into accommodating them.

Or perhaps their expertise or position in your organisation grants them so much power that the disruption caused by changing things would outweigh the collateral damage they are currently causing. Instead of trying to change things, you could choose to rebuild or re-arrange the way your organisation works to adapt it to the demands of your Scary Specialist.

You wouldn't be the first leader I've worked with who made the pragmatic decision to try and do this. But make sure you're not just putting off one of the other options while trying (and failing) to cushion the rest of the business from the fallout.

Here are some steps you might want to take:

1 Ensure that your Scary Specialist is always surrounded by highly competent team members. Help them to recruit only the best to their team, and be as sure as you can be that those recruits will perform well straight out of the box.

2 Check that all the supporting processes, resources and support staff who help them to deliver are functioning well and are aligned to the objectives of the Scary Specialist's domain.

3 Make sure that you, or somebody with influence, is doing the strategic, big-picture, long-term thinking about where your organisation is going and how well it responds to its marketplace. Your Scary Specialist may not automatically do this, with their focus instead on polishing performance.

Become a bit more scary yourself

Part of your leadership task might be to raise the stakes far enough that your Scary Specialist really understands that it's time to change their behaviour. Then they can bring themselves to address their unconscious fears and the lack of wider vision that keeps them repeating undesirable behaviours.

It may not get to the point where formal disciplinary procedures are called for, but be prepared to get very directive about things – making it clear that they need to change or else suffer your wrath.

Points to consider include the following:

- Make sure you're confident about how your organisation's formal disciplinary process works and that there is appropriate support to help you with it. Your Scary Specialist will sit up and pay attention to your competence with this.

- Might the withdrawal of your personal approval or even a no-nonsense personal intervention from you be enough? Your aim is to be absolutely clear about what behaviours are not acceptable, what you expect to see in their place and how you'll monitor the situation.

- Difficult people don't usually just become difficult in a vacuum – are there other pressures behind these behaviours? Who or what is colluding with or contributing to the situation, and how will becoming scary yourself impact those?

Get them to raise their game

The third strategy for leading a Scary Specialist away from being difficult is to use their own natural strengths. They value competence and they like things to run like a well-oiled machine. But if their behaviours are causing problems in the rest of the organisation, that's a huge *incompetence*.

In this situation, they're like a Formula 1 pit crew who can change the tyres better and faster than anyone – but only at the cost of damaging the rest of the car, or even losing the overall race.

Your leadership task here has three aspects:

1 To make it clear what the stakes are and how important it is that they grasp the development opportunity you're offering them

2 To raise their awareness upwards and outwards, so that they genuinely comprehend the wider negative impacts of how they're behaving

3 To shift their blame-based approach towards unsatisfactory things which are outside their immediate domain, to one where they join in to take mutual responsibility and accountability for them.

None of these are easy things for a Scary Specialist to do, since they will go out of their way to avoid areas in which they feel incompetent or lacking in direct control.

New competencies which will support these changes are set out in more detail in the Growth tips section at the end of this chapter.

Tips for colleagues and staff of Scary Specialists

Working for or alongside a Scary Specialist can be a satisfying experience when things are going well. You can focus on getting things done efficiently, effectively and to a rewardingly high standard. Relationships will feel professional and it can be a great chance to learn deeper skills and to show just what you can do.

But when things aren't going well, and your Scary Specialist feels that their independence or their ability to deliver or manage their domain to the right standard is threatened, working as their colleague or team member can be a very unpleasant experience!

In those circumstances, there are four important tactics you can deploy to change the situation.

Raise your own game

Every tough situation is an opportunity for self-development, even if it's painful and unfair. But start with yourself anyway – after all, the only person we truly have direct control over is ourselves.

Ask yourself these questions – don't be self-critical, just open. At this point most people in a Difficult person situation will have already asked 'Is it me?' anyway, so take a moment to do a more objective assessment of that:

- Is there something which you should be delivering but aren't?
- Could you genuinely be bringing down the pace or quality of the Scary Specialist's department?

If you can truly and honestly answer yes to either of these questions, then act on them. Increase your pace, learn the new skill that is needed and re-dedicate yourself – but first make sure you also check out the tactics below.

Don't suffer alone or in silence

Working with a Scary Specialist who is being difficult can be bruising, bullying and scary! Leaders and organisations can sometimes collude in this – letting them get away with behaviour that isn't acceptable, because of the value of their expertise. The more of us who suffer this alone or in silence, the easier it is for leaders and organisations to look the other way. Make sure you're doing most or even all of the following if you're in that situation:

- **Tell friends and colleagues.** There's no shame in being on the receiving end of somebody else's bad behaviour. It isn't your fault, it doesn't make you weak and it's absolutely the right time to look for support.

- **Get help and advice.** Look to your human resources colleagues, to your own leader if the Scary Specialist is a colleague of yours, or to a professional, trade or other association. Ask what support is available to you. Ask who in your organisation is responsible for changing this situation.

- **Tell them.** In situations where there's a real power imbalance, for example if the Scary Specialist is your boss, it can be actually career-threatening to shine the light on their bad behaviour. Work doesn't need to be like that though, and it shouldn't be like that, and whatever the outcome, you'll eventually thank yourself for not tolerating the unacceptable. A typical Scary Specialist may not even be aware of the impact they're having. Put it in these kinds of terms: 'I'm not happy with how you sometimes behave towards me. Here are X specific things you've done recently and here's how I felt as a result . . . Here's what I need from you instead . . . .' The points here about boundaries may also help with this.

Boundaries

Scary Specialists value competence, drive and independence. When those things are reflected back to them as qualities in other people they will generally respect them and understand how to engage and interact with them.

So get clear about your own boundaries, and then clearly and boldly live and work to those boundaries. In addition to keeping you whole, this is a great way to signal that you are someone it's worth being an ally of – and not someone to antagonise or work against.

Consider these issues to help define your own boundaries:

- What kind of conditions are important to you at work?

- What sort of behaviours or approaches are not acceptable to you?

- What do you need to say 'No' to?

- What practical things might help define some boundaries for you – hours/time, space, money, resources, etc.?

- What else is a boundary for you – perhaps either a no-go or a must-have of some kind?

- Make sure that the things which sustain you, which keep you healthy, happy and balanced, are not getting crowded out.

Put your boundaries into practice. Say no when you need to. Ask for what you do need. Trust yourself and what you believe to be important. Be prepared to walk away if necessary.

Stay connected

Like all of the types on the Disconnection row of my matrix, Scary Specialists have a tendency to separate their domain from the rest of the organisation.

For example, as a member of their staff, they may insist that leaders in other departments address requests and other approaches only through them – and not directly to you. But you can and should have ongoing informal and social contact with people from other parts of your organisation. Similarly, stay in contact with developments in the wider sphere in which your organisation operates – go to conferences, attend learning events. Make and maintain connections wherever you can.

As a colleague of a Scary Specialist, make sure that you're not automatically or unconsciously avoiding connections with them and their department. Or that you're not using their typical 'go away' response as an excuse to dodge the thorny issue of how to include them in wider discussions and considerations. Keep trying to keep the connection going!

Growth tips for Scary Specialists

As a leader-mentor, a coach or a human resources professional, here are the main points to cover in creating a targeted development strategy for a Scary Specialist.

Resistance to overcome

My experience in coaching Scary Specialists is that they've rarely self-referred to me. More often, I'm walking into a room or onto a video call with someone who is only there because other powerful stakeholders have strongly suggested they should be. That sets up an interesting dynamic with a person whose resistance to change is often already pretty high! Use the following points as a checklist before you start your work with a Scary Specialist:

1 **Competence** – they will be alert for any signs that you might not know what you're doing or might not have a tried and tested approach to dealing with this situation.

2 **Expertise** – I've heard several comments from Scary Specialists that one-size-fits-all development or disciplinary processes are

not suitable, and they have very been critical of internal human resources staff who aren't prepared for this type of nuanced resistance.

3 **Time** – they may say that you're 'wasting their time' looking for soft-skills development needs that won't help to deliver their work outputs. Make sure you're clear that this is their responsibility not yours and is happening because their overall ability to get the job done is *already* being compromised by the difficulties that others are experiencing in working with them.

Mindset shifts

One of the behavioural strategies that will have helped a Scary Specialist to be successful in the past is, unsurprisingly, to become more specialised. That approach is a bit like the groove in a vinyl record: the more you play it, the deeper the groove gets. So mindset shifts can take a bit of work with this type of difficult person. Here's what to explore:

- **Shame** – in this context shame is the gap between how we feel we *are* perceived and how we really *want* to be perceived. Scary Specialists may have buried their true feelings about how colleagues find them unlikeable. Ask them: if there was a way of being so good at their work without rubbing people up the wrong way, would they adopt it?

- **Self-sabotage** – in this context, self-sabotage is the unconscious pattern that makes sure any attempt to change will fail before it's even started. Coach them to be more self-aware by looking out for when they say things like this:
  - 'I don't have the time/authority/resources to do anything about X.'
  - 'That's just the way things are around here.'
  More self-awareness is often all it takes to break this pattern.

- **Blame** – Scary Specialists can sometimes unconsciously protect themselves from getting distracted or overloaded by blaming others when things don't go right. Raise their self-awareness of this by listening out for when they say things like:

- 'If it wasn't for the terrible computer system/that incompetent person/the bad decisions by the board/etc. everything would be great.'

And then coach them around the impact of blaming, as it can take away their own responsibility and power for actually getting those things fixed. What one action could they take that might actually help instead of just blaming?

Skills to develop

When offering suggestions to a Scary Specialist about which new skills they might want to develop, highlight their strengths around 'competency'. They already know how to acquire skills and how to become really good at things. Now it's time to apply that strength to become competent in some new areas. The Matrix of Difficult People helps us to identify the three most useful areas to focus on.

From the attention focus dimension of the matrix, where Scary Specialists have a task focus, there are two areas to consider:

1 Skills in the long-term, visionary leadership that comes from having a wider, systems focus on the organisation and its marketplace. This helps to position their own work and department as part of something bigger and helps them to see how to contribute to that bigger picture.

2 Skills in coaching and developing other people. This helps them to have an alternative strategy for dealing with people who aren't immediately able to become top performers (other than their more common approach of just avoiding or getting rid of such people).

From the stress strategy dimension of the matrix, where Scary Specialists have a disconnection strategy:

Perhaps their biggest growth and development could come from not separating themselves and their domain quite so much. From not disconnecting from those people who are outside their safe circle of trust, respect and control. Instead, they might choose to develop the kind of soft skills a good chairperson needs, for example listening, consensus-building and group decision-making.

Summary

Competence, drive and independence – they're great qualities, aren't they?

You may have used the services of somebody with qualities like these. Somebody specialised in what they do, who has built up their knowledge and expertise over years of study and work.

As a customer, client, patient or other recipient of their services, you were almost certainly pleased with what they did. What you may not know is that for their boss, their colleagues and their staff, the experience of working alongside this type of person can, in the wrong circumstances, be very different indeed. In those circumstances, they can become a Scary Specialist. Someone who can become extremely challenging, obstructive and brutally critical, either openly or on the sly.

Leading a Scary Specialist at those times can be a choice between re-arranging things around them, so that they can continue to deliver, or out-scaring them, to the point where they'll be open to the need for change. If you do that well, you can re-direct their natural strengths to develop more rounded competencies. You can raise their awareness and help them adjust their focus so that they make a positive contribution to the leadership of the whole organisation as well as just their own domain.

Working alongside a Scary Specialist as a colleague or team member can be exhilarating when things are going well. It's a chance to develop your own abilities to the maximum, to be part of a well-oiled machine. Make sure you don't fall into the cogs of that machine though. You need to be at the top of your game and you need to make sure that you know where your boundaries are. And to look after those boundaries and your overall balance in life and work. When you sense that a boundary is being crossed, it's important not to suffer in silence, but to look for support and allies. Lastly, make sure you don't follow the lead of your Scary Specialist and become disconnected from the wider organisation and the world outside it – instead, stay connected.

For those human resources specialists, coaches and mentor-leaders who want to help with the development needs of a Scary Specialist, you'd better be as competent in your field as they are in theirs. Get past their resistance, and you can be vital in helping them uncover important feelings about how they really want to be perceived. You can help them shift counterproductive thought patterns about how to deal with, instead of just complaining about, those issues that are outside their direct control. And you can point them towards acquiring new skills that will make those shifts possible and enable them to develop, not discard, those people who need more support before they can become as competent.

With the approach suggested in this chapter we can have a Scary Specialist who is no longer scary. They can expand their competences, becoming an expert at working *with* others instead of despite them. And as well as keeping their independence and authenticity intact, they can show others how to apply similar levels of drive for results and quality in a way that will benefit the whole organisation.

In the next chapter, we'll consider a related type of difficult person at work – the Dark Strategist.

Note

1 Martin, Steve (n.d.), as cited in Nash, Jennie, 'Be so good they can't ignore you', Medium. Last accessed 22 June 2023.

chapter 11

Type 2 – The Dark Strategist

'Everyone has a plan. Until they get punched in the mouth.'

Mike Tyson[1]

In a nutshell

The Dark Strategist is usually someone who likes having a grand plan and will work behind the scenes to perfect it.

Key characteristics: They are insightful and ambitious, driven to figure out all that's required to achieve a key goal or to realise a step-change in the business.

Why others can find them difficult: Issues at work can arise when they've tried to move people and partner organisations around without question or autonomy, treating others like chess pieces as they try to deliver their plan.

Example

Ian has always been good at seeing the big picture. People say that he's usually two or three steps ahead whenever there's a problem or an opportunity that might affect the company's success. He's ambitious but sometimes feels that a top job such as managing director would make him too visible. He can get very frustrated when people need explanations or discussions before they'll agree to do what he wants.

At their best

Dark Strategists are insightful leaders, figuring out what needs to happen and mastering a deep understanding of the issues, trends, choices – and people – involved. They combine an ability to see how the component parts of a plan and/or an organisation could mesh together, and to strategise from that viewpoint, with precise execution and an ability to bring people with them. They often carry a big ambition, not necessarily about themselves, but about fulfilling the organisation's potential.

When do things get difficult?

The Dark Strategist has a strong need to understand how everything fits together. They believe that somewhere there is a perfect plan which incorporates all the opportunities and strengths and solves all the weaknesses and threats. And if other people would also understand and accept such a plan for themselves, and then carry it out without dragging the Dark Strategist down into the details, things would be great.

But that's often not the case and Dark Strategists can sometimes hit a real rough patch at work if they face a 'wicked' problem or opportunity. One for which there may be no single clear answer but which requires an on-going dialogue and compromise with other people and organisations over whom they have no direct control.

Their place in the Matrix of Difficult People

	T	S	P
D	😠	🤯	😇
E	😡	🙂	😎
A	😬	😐	😳

Attention Focus

Systems focused – the Dark Strategist's primary focus, and the lens through which they assess things, is on interconnected systems and how those mesh together.

Stress Strategy

Disconnection – under pressure, the Dark Strategist will tend to withdraw from those they don't trust or can't control and disconnect from demands to explain or persuade.

How to spot a Dark Strategist

Secret, solitary planning

Under stress, they may withdraw and start working on a grand plan alone, with no way of getting it into action and then becoming overwhelmed and isolated.

At those times, others may experience them as cold and aloof, keeping the answers to themselves and not developing the emotional bonds that make things run smoothly. There may be a sense that they have locked themselves in a quiet room in a remote location.

One-way information flows and a lack of detail

You might notice unexpected delays in delivery or unforeseen requests for more information. But that information flow may only be working one way and you may also feel excluded when you'd perhaps like them to take time to explain what the plan is, or to ask your views on the approach that's being taken. You may also notice that the detail hasn't been worked through and that you are then expected to solve any practical problems that don't fit into the neatness of the framework.

Manipulation and criticism

They may attempt to gain covert control, manoeuvring in the shadows to get power, with potentially damaging results. When they already have or gain power they may treat some people and partners like chess pieces and try to direct their efforts without getting buy-in, without making their plans available and transparent, or without gaining a broad enough consensus.

People and partner organisations may report feeling manipulated. Information may have been withheld, which restricts the range of options available. Key choices about resources may have already been taken without consultation. The Dark Strategist is also likely to be highly critical of those who don't understand (in their view) how the issues and the plan all join up, sometimes describing those people as too slow, stupid or resistant.

Tips for leaders of a Dark Strategist

A well-developed Dark Strategist can be one of the most powerful people to have on your team. With the right leadership they can readily tackle some of the most important functions of senior management, including problem-solving, operational delivery and role modelling critical thinking skills.

Getting them to that point, however, or turning them around when they've hit a rough patch, can be quite a challenge because of their tendencies to be manipulative and secretive and their ability to think two steps ahead.

On the outside, it may look as if the kind of joined-up analysis, thinking and planning that a Dark Strategist does so well comes easily to them. Compared to others, this may be true, but the price is often a need for quiet, intense and solitary reflection. Their threads of thought may feel easily broken, solutions elusive and the correct sequence of execution easily lost. Where other people may not worry that there is no overarching, cohesive and elegant model that perfectly describes the situation, a Dark Strategist will be very uncomfortable without one.

In addition to the development suggestions at the end of this chapter, here are the aspects of your leadership that can be most helpful in getting a Dark Strategist back on track and keeping their less-useful tendencies in check.

Role model inclusive collaboration

Show them what it looks like to tackle problems in a group, including these steps:

- Use facilitation skills and tools so that teams can collaboratively address problems and examine ways of working together.

- Look for opportunities to present your own ideas in a group forum that includes your Dark Strategist.

- Show them it's possible to invite feedback and discuss alternatives to your ideas without being precious or feeling threatened by the process.

- Discuss to what extent they need to adopt a kind of 'go-and-come-back' approach – some solitary thinking time that must then also be endorsed in a group session. If they need this, allow extra time for it in the deliverables that you agree.

The map is not the territory

There's a saying I sometimes use in my coaching: 'The map is not the territory.' The usefulness of a map, or the model of an organisation or a problem, is not that it perfectly describes the situation, but that it allows for exploration.

A map that completely represented what you might find on the ground would have to be so large and detailed that it would be unusable. Instead, it's a tool that helps us to picture things in the abstract so that we can broadly understand where we are, see where we want to get to and know how that journey relates to the other things around us.

Leaders of Dark Strategists should become familiar with the types of models that help organisations to identify their place in their market, develop strategies and allocate resources. This will give you a common language and a way of connecting as well as, crucially, allowing you to make sure that devising the perfect model doesn't become their end goal. Instead, encourage them to use such models and plans as tools to help people focus and deliver collaboratively.

Done is better than perfect

We all know this saying by now. Done is better than perfect because it avoids paralysis by analysis, gives real-world learning and feedback that can be incorporated into the next iteration and is the only step that actually delivers value and/or sales.

But in some places, the culture will actively punish people for delivering anything less than perfect.

Dark Strategists aren't always perfectionists, but they are really good at predicting the consequences of producing something that doesn't quite do all that it could. If those consequences are negative – either because of your organisation's culture or because of something they've thought of that others haven't – your Dark Strategist is likely to delay and tinker more than might be useful.

Leaders should consider whether there are cultural barriers to their Dark Strategist adopting a 'done is better than perfect' approach and what support or shielding they might need to help them get on and deliver.

People aren't chess pieces

This is a good aspect of their leadership for you to work on with your Dark Strategist. Have an open and frank series of conversations about how they relate to others, including:

- Reflecting together on whether they might have a tendency to try and move team members and partner organisations around like chess pieces.

- Asking them to figure out for themselves how they might connect with others more as individual people.

- Showing them what it looks like to be more collaborative, so that they can achieve consensus in teams and groups by encouraging participation.

- Helping them to put people first when appropriate, so that they know how to create harmony, build emotional bonds, and motivate and support, rather than manipulate, individual people and teams. There are more tips on this in the Growth section at the end of this chapter.

Tips for colleagues and staff of Dark Strategists

Your experience of working for or alongside a Dark Strategist will depend a lot on what kind of person you are and on how far their traits have tipped over into the difficult realm.

If things are going well, you'll benefit from their insights and their ability to think ahead. You'll also get to play a part as they brilliantly execute their master plan. If things are going badly, you may find that your needs for inclusion, recognition and autonomy are either not met or are rudely discounted. And you may be involuntarily excluded or manipulated. Overall, it's unlikely to be as threatening as some of the other types – just insufficient, difficult to manage and demotivating!

The tips below will help in all of the situations described above, so either work through them in order or just cherry-pick the ones that feel most relevant now.

Don't look to them to fulfil your attention needs

If you're someone who needs personal feedback and recognition, and you don't have a systems focus like they do, the experience of working for or alongside a Dark Strategist may be an unsatisfactory one – they've sometimes been described as a 'cold fish'.

Good leaders act as a coach to people, listening to their concerns and ambitions, giving empathy and support, celebrating their contribution and respecting who they are, at the same time as giving them appropriate challenges. And a Dark Strategist who has become difficult may not even realise that others find all of this helpful. This can leave you feeling that you're weak for having that need (you're not) or resentful and let-down and can contribute to a big gap in your motivation.

Find others to help get the personal recognition and attention you need. For example, hire an external coach or join something like a learning and development set at work.

Stay or become well connected

Everybody who works for or with a difficult person who is on the *Disconnection* row of the matrix will find it useful to adopt a similar tactic to this. Always keep the lines of communication to other parts of the organisation, to other teams and individuals as open as you possibly can. Build alliances, develop information sources, and contribute to any cross-functional projects that you can.

If your Dark Strategist is being really difficult, you're going to have to compensate for two related problems: their tendency to keep you in the dark; and their failure to listen to your viewpoint. For the latter, when there's an important issue that you feel is being ignored because it doesn't fit with their plan, you may need to find ways to safely influence around them and bring those issues to the attention of others. See also the next point about boundaries.

Boundaries

Boundary management is always an important tactic when you're dealing with a difficult person. It concerns being really clear about what's acceptable to you in the way that others behave at work and what isn't. A Dark Strategist can sometimes regard people who don't quickly and comprehensively understand how systems and inter-related issues mesh together as stupid. And they may actually say this, or at least make it obvious that's what they think. Don't tolerate this kind of behaviour. Call them out on it and explicitly request something else.

For example, *'I'm feeling belittled. What I actually need is a clear explanation of how this will work, in a way that makes sense to me.'*

Demand involvement and/or autonomy

You might find that a Dark Strategist is closed or even hostile towards any competing ideas and frameworks. As a colleague or a team member, your suggestions, ideas or requests for input to or dialogue about a structure or a plan etc. are likely to be rejected or even just ignored.

Demand the involvement and/or autonomy that you need. 'Demand' is a strong word but you may find you have to make your case pretty strongly so that it can't be ignored or overlooked. A Dark Strategist's tendency to exclude people and to move them around like chess pieces isn't meant to be malicious. It's just their way of coping with what feels like a fragile, hard-to-grasp process that they absolutely need to get 'right', although it can feel rough if you're on the receiving end. For this reason it is worth trying to change things. Stay reasonable and see how assertive you can be. For example:

- *'I want to be involved in the planning for this project. It's part of my job and it can't be done properly without consulting me and the area I represent.'*

- *'That decision isn't one that reflects my goals. I want some say in how this will work because it's going to affect me.'*

Actions speak louder than words – so read the map

A really proactive person can be a great ally for a Dark Strategist, who can be more drawn to the neatness of a plan than to the execution of it. If you love getting on with stuff, have some intention and forethought to your actions. In particular:

- Make sure you act in accordance with the big picture or the plan.
- Consider the appropriate sequence of actions – what needs to happen first; what shouldn't be done just yet?

You'll win lots of trust and a paradoxical amount of autonomy from a Dark Strategist if you adopt this kind of approach.

Upskill your strategic thinking

If you haven't already developed your own skills at thinking strategically, that might also be an area to consider. What you explore will depend on your business or organisation's priorities, but could include:

- What are the basic kinds of choices in the ways that organisations in different industries are structured?
- How do businesses and other organisations define their market-place? And what are the factors that determine whether they will be successful in that market?
- How do terms like Mission, Vision and Strategy get used in your organisation?

When I worked for a Dark Strategist, I asked them to recommend some books and other resources that covered the kind of thinking and issues we were dealing with at work. Just that request led to a positive shift in our working relationship.

Growth tips for Dark Strategists

What if you also have some responsibility for dealing with the professional development of a Dark Strategist at work? You might be a coach, a leader-mentor or a human resources professional.

You should start with the big picture because that's how they'll most likely want to approach it. Think of their development needs as being part of a system and create a plan from there. Maybe even something with a diagram or a model, because that is most likely to engage them.

If you already have a development model or a leadership framework in your organisation, use that. If not, there's a really simple one below for Dark Strategists. Let them go away and design a more tailored one for themselves if they want to.

Make the bigger picture more concrete and less abstract

People don't exist in a vacuum at work. They share an inter-connected system, with lots of moving parts, many of which aren't even within the boundaries of your organisation. Dark Strategists are often people who intuitively get this, but perhaps in an overly abstract way. They're often very responsible, driven to understand all those moving parts and to make the most of them, not just for themselves but for the whole organisation. It can help them to start seeing this in terms of actual people who need to be considered and actual tasks that need to be done. You could simply discuss the following, seeking always to be as tangible as possible about it:

- Who are the key people that are dependent on them?
- Who else is impacted by their work – and in what way? Be specific.
- What's their current work priority; and why?
- Why are you both having this discussion about their develop-ment? Be frank. What led to it? What's involved? What tangible steps will happen as a result of this? See also the point here about execution.

Stay connected

Their stress strategy is one of *Disconnection* and this is worth discussing in a similarly open and simple way. Here are some prompts to help them explore:

- Are they aware that they might be separating themselves from those they don't trust or can't control and disconnecting from explaining or managing the detail?
- If they put themselves in other people's shoes, what might that disconnection look and feel like to those people?
- What impact does it have?

- If they wanted to have more connection and still be able to do what they do, what would first have to happen? And how would they know if it had worked?

Relating to people as individual people

It's my belief that Dark Strategists are often overwhelmed by the complexity of other people's needs and preferences. And this is why they sometimes ignore people as people and simply treat them as chess pieces.

The trick for Dark Strategists is not to try and master that complexity, but to get out of their comfort zone of systematising and to be really practical about it. Here are some points they could explore:

- Stop expecting other people to do things just because you told them to; most need something more than that.

- To find out what other people are feeling, what they want, or what their viewpoint is; practice just asking them.

- If there's something you've asked people to do, and they seem unable or reluctant, is it possible to go and get stuck in alongside them? Sometimes leaders need to collaborate on a very practical, detailed level like that. Even if it's just to learn more about what that person's day-to-day working life is like.

Execution, execution, execution

I've written earlier in this chapter about 'Done is better than perfect'. Dark Strategists often have a tendency to avoid inconvenient detail and messy but necessary action. For those supporting the development of a Dark Strategist, it can often help to get into that kind of nitty-gritty earlier rather than later. For example:

- What are the practical steps they are taking to implement the plan?

- What will be the first instance of the rubber actually hitting the road?

- Which three tangible outcomes will show that something is actually happening?

Check whether two-way communication is working

Perhaps the hardest thing for Dark Strategists to learn is to wait long enough for others to catch up with their understanding of a situation. This is often a question of patience and of communication. There aren't really any shortcuts to this, but there is a handy six-step process they can build into everything they do, which will help to speed it up and make it more effective:

1 Always plan for a communication stage.

2 Find a way to check that people have (a) understood and (b) agreed with you.

3 If either (a) or (b) above aren't happening, consider it as a failure to communicate effectively (in both directions), rather than a failure to understand.

4 Listen carefully to any feedback – listening is a key part of communicating.

5 Adjust the plan accordingly.

6 Find a new way to communicate the issues.

Repeat until successful!

Summary

- -

If I visualise a Dark Strategist, I'm sometimes a little reminded of the Emperor in the Star Wars movies. This is unfairly negative because the hidden machinations this person uses have always seemed to me to have a very positive intention behind them. A drive to sort out a complicated problem at work or to get all the pieces of the business in place for an important opportunity, often combined with great foresight and understanding.

When they've learned to flex their natural systems approach to also include people and tasks, they can be insightful leaders. And when they've also learned to control their stress strategy, so that instead of *disconnecting* when things get tough they collaborate more and make room for others to participate more, they can be really powerful leaders too.

But without that learning, it can all go horribly wrong. At those times, faced with a wickedly complex issue they may stay in the dark, plotting away. Only emerging to try and manoeuvre or even bully people into unquestioningly following their instructions.

Leading a Dark Strategist effectively can be a test of your ability to speak their language and strategise with them, combined with a crucial need to coach and role-model different ways of approaching things. Some priorities are transactional, making sure they get stuff done as well as planning and modelling it. Other priorities are about encouraging and coaxing them to connect with a wider range of other people, *as* people.

Working alongside a Dark Strategist can be a very good experience if you can think strategically *and* you can work out how to influence what goes into their thinking *and* you don't mind getting little or no recognition. If not, you'll have to get your recognition needs met elsewhere, make sure you stay well connected when your Dark Strategist might disconnect, and be as reasonably assertive as you can to manage your own boundaries and demand to be involved.

The development process for a Dark Strategist usually has to start by connecting the abstract big picture to a more concrete reality. The remaining priorities for their development are then about helping them to stay connected when under pressure, encouraging them to treat others both as individuals and as people to collaborate with, executing strategy as well as planning it and, finally, making sure they allow time to communicate effectively, including listening to feedback.

With the tactics and steps set out in this chapter, a Dark Strategist can become someone who leads with a great understanding of the people and issues involved at work. Someone who can both have a unique perspective on the big picture *and* deliver the right set of outcomes in productive collaboration with others.

In the next chapter we'll meet a different type of difficult person at work. Someone whose positive qualities and strong principles can themselves be the cause of difficulties – the Martyr.

Note

1 Tyson, Mike (n.d.), as cited in 'Everybody has a plan until they get punched in the mouth. - How did the famous Mike Tyson quote originate?', Sportskeeda. Last accessed 22 June 2023.

chapter 12

Type 3 – The Martyr

'When I let go of what I am, I become
what I might be.'

Lao Tzu[1]

In a nutshell

The Martyr is usually a highly principled person, with a strong sense of justice and a clear belief that things should be improved for the betterment of all.

Key characteristics: This person has an extremely high work ethic and a profound care for others. They often inspire deep loyalty in their followers.

Why others can find them difficult: Issues at work can arise from their refusal to compromise for an imperfect solution, from the judgements they make about others whom they see as less principled, and from the self-sacrifice and inability to progress that this can lead to.

Example

Rachael works harder than almost anybody else. Some say she's uncompromising and tough to live up to – and others find her seriously inspirational. She's never run away from a demanding job, especially when something important needs doing which affects a lot of people. If she doesn't regard you as a good person you'll probably feel it, but might not know for sure until you realise that she's cut you out of the loop.

At their best

Martyrs are transformative leaders who will seek out wide-scale and deep-reaching improvements. They act selflessly in service of customers, clients or end users. They are the kind of person who makes you sigh with relief when they arrive; prepared to tackle issues that previously seemed insurmountable. The genuine and deep care they direct towards their individual team members inspires great loyalty – and, at their best, they have learned to apply this upwards and sideways as well, influencing and strategising with great skill.

When do things get difficult?

The Martyr is driven to do things 'right' – either according to principle or to the letter of their commitment. They expect a similarly high level of principle and work ethic from others and assume that others are equally committed to the cause.

The situation in which things become difficult at work around a Martyr involves a combination of:

- A large, complex challenge
- A board or a management team who are not quite cognisant of all the implications of that challenge; and
- A workforce under pressure and who they feel needs looking after.

Under stress in that kind of situation they may attempt to implement the 'right' solution using only the resources they directly control. They are likely to become very critical and untrusting of their bosses and colleagues. When tasked with implementing changes or taking action that they judge to be unfair or expedient, or which won't be enough to solve the whole issue, they can find it difficult to make any headway. They may sacrifice their own work–life balance and health.

Their place in the Matrix of Difficult People

	T	S	P
D			
E			
A			

Attention Focus

People focused – the Martyr's primary focus is on people: their thoughts, feelings and social needs. They will assess a work project in terms of its impact on people, both internal and external to the organisation.

Stress Strategy

Disconnection – under pressure, the Martyr will tend to separate themselves too much, turning their backs on those that they no longer trust.

How to spot a Martyr

Indirect criticism

If a Martyr has effectively turned their back on their bosses and colleagues, you may not get that much interaction with them – which is an indication in itself. When you do interact, you may be left feeling slightly judged or found wanting. As if you have somehow failed to live up to high-enough levels of principle, integrity and work ethic.

Listen out for their indirectly critical comments or questions to you, especially things like:

- *'But how will that solve X?'* or
- *'But that doesn't address the impact on Y group of people!'*

Defensive cordon

You may get a sense, either from the inside or the outside of it, that the Martyr has thrown up a defensive cordon around their people. On the outside, bosses and colleagues may notice that they are denied direct access to those people. On the inside, some people may feel that the Martyr is carrying the lame ducks – covering for short-falls in some people's abilities or attitudes.

No compromise; no progress

Martyrs can sometimes fail to make progress even on projects to which they are highly committed. This is because they may not be influencing upwards and sideways effectively since they can be uncompromising with others whom they see as less principled. Additionally, they may not have developed their systems thinking – so they don't know *why* or *how* to compromise strategically, when some compromise may be required to at least achieve something.

If you experience indirect push-back against a suggested solution, or you see that no progress is being made (when it could be if one or other criteria were relaxed), you may have a Martyr at the helm.

Tips for leaders of a Martyr

A Martyr who has overcome their disconnection stress strategy and learned to turn some of their people focus upwards and outwards can be a forceful and reassuring presence on your team. With development, they'll be able to strategically influence people in authority, removing the roadblocks that will then enable them and their followers to really get things done.

Reaching that goal, however, can be quite a challenge for leaders. You'll need to influence and include them just when they are most likely to be mistrusting and making negative judgements about you. It's also important to remember that Martyrs are not quite as fearless as they might seem and that their courage is external, coming from their desire to support a principle.

In addition to the growth tips at the end of this chapter, here are some of the steps that will help you to unlock the real power of a Martyr.

Reveal your own principles

More than anything a Martyr wants to know that their leaders are themselves principled people; that they stand for something – especially if that is of benefit to others. So tell them:

- What are the values or principles that you bring to *your* work?

- How are those of benefit to the other people in your business; and to the end users of your product or service?

- When have you been able to demonstrate that you live and work by those principles or values; and when did you fail to live up to them?

If you sense that your Martyr may already have turned their back on you, you may need to do this in a bridge-building way. Make it personal: *'I'd like us to build a stronger working relationship. Let's meet off-site and grab a coffee together.'* And in sharing your own values: *'I don't think I've mentioned some of what's important to me in the way I approach my own work . . . '*

Bring them into the bigger agenda

Martyrs sometimes fail to grasp the wider context in which your business or organisation operates. They may overlook the external constraints and influences you face that have an impact on what is possible. In an ideal world, that wouldn't be the case, and you'd be able to have a free hand, letting your Martyr implement an uncompromised solution. But businesses and organisations don't exist in a vacuum. Turn it around, so that they can't blame you for not existing in a perfect world and instead must become part of a solution that may involve compromise.

Include them when discussing that wider context and setting the strategic agenda, covering these points:

- What are the constraints that you face?
- How does the work you've asked your Martyr to lead on contribute to the wider agenda?
- Where are the points at which compromises might have to be made?
- Who are the external stakeholders and influencers that also need to be satisfied?

Issues around failure culture and self-sacrifice

I mentioned earlier that Martyrs may need to be tutored on those external factors that require a compromise solution. But I've also seen situations where boards and management committees have asked someone to implement something without *themselves* having thought through the implications. Because of their natural style Martyrs will not try to compromise and may not tell you about any roadblocks they've identified in case it seems like failure.

Martyrs present as strong people. But their principles and strengths can mask and are often driven by a real worry about what might happen if they fail. They may worry about the consequences of not delivering a perfect solution; about the impacts this will have on others and about what it says about the kind of person they want to be. This worry may be behind the Martyr's disconnection stress strategy and can lead to them sacrificing their work–life balance and health.

To tackle these issues, leaders should consider three related areas. First, have you or your board set them up to fail?

- Is what you've asked of them really possible without a compromise that you wouldn't actually be prepared to accept?
- Are there external constraints and influences over which your Martyr has no control, but which you may have overlooked?

If so, these are issues that need to be addressed at the right level and in the right forum, and may not be entirely within the remit of your Martyr to deal with.

Second, consider your business's attitude to failure and how this might affect the area you've tasked your Martyr to work on:

- What is acceptable to fail at, in your organisation?
- And what is unacceptable?
- How does your business approach the concept of 'failing forward' – that even if not everything is achieved, something will have been and other things will have been learned in the process too?

Again, have these discussions openly, at the right and highest level possible. Get the culture right and people like your Martyr will feel safe enough to deliver great change in an open and collaborative way.

Third, encourage them to voice their worries and address their balance:

- What are they afraid of, in terms of the outcomes of their work and the implications that failure has for them personally?
- What impact does this have on their balance and their health?

Often just getting these things out in the open is enough to make a real difference. Make sure you support and encourage better balance so that they are not tempted to self-sacrifice for their principles.

Tips for colleagues and staff of a Martyr

It's unlikely that you'll have a seriously bad experience of working for or with a Martyr, but there can be some significant consequential fall-out to be very wary of. At the least, colleagues may feel frustrated, judged and excluded. Team members may find they are denied exposure and development opportunities, are held back from advancement and may suffer by association. Here are my tactics for successfully working with or alongside a Martyr.

When access is denied

You may notice that a Martyr colleague is denying you access to their team members and requiring you to direct requests only through them, creating a critical bottleneck for you or your team.

If this is happening it's likely to be a sign that you have lost their trust, either because of something you did (or didn't) do, or because you are seen as being on the side of a boss they don't feel safe with. To respond well to this:

- Ask for personal time together, demonstrating that people as individuals are important to you.

- Share something around your own principles and values, which helps them see that you operate from a similar principled approach, even if some of your principles and values are different from theirs.

- Talk about the worries and concerns around having greater integration between your respective team members. In particular, what do they feel that their team members need protecting from and how could you help alleviate that?

You will probably need to take the initiative on this, but once you do, it's likely to be well received.

Set boundaries to being judged or criticised

Colleagues of Martyrs can often feel judged or find themselves being criticised about either their work ethic or their integrity, or both!

It isn't acceptable for a colleague to treat you this way, even if they are someone who is themselves highly principled and has a tremendous work ethic. To suggest that your unwillingness to sacrifice your own work–life balance is a weakness or deficiency is wrong. To imply that you have shown a lack of principle because you've been flexible in dealing with complex issues that require compromise is also wrong.

Deal with this in a straightforward way at a personal meeting:

- *'You said (or did) X. The impact of this on me was that I felt [judged/ criticised] for being [lazy/unscrupulous]. I'd like to talk about why this has happened and how we might work together better. But first, I want to ask you not to [respond to me/treat me] in that way in future.'*

Stay connected

A Martyr is another difficult person on the *Disconnection* row of my matrix and anybody who works with or for someone on that row will want to adopt a tactic like this. Stay connected with other people outside your department. Keep the lines of communication open to other parts of the organisation. Without doing this, you limit what is possible for you and your work, especially at those times when the Martyr's tendency is to turn their back on the rest of the business.

If necessary, ask for permission to work on building those connections, although my experience has been that it's better when working with a Martyr to just go ahead and do it.

Proactively manage your career

Because Martyrs have a tendency to disconnect and then throw up this protective cordon around their department and team, there can be a few side effects for those on the inside. These include the following:

- You may not be getting stretched if your Martyr is carrying too much of the load themselves.

- Your Martyr may not be working to persuade other stakeholders that key pieces of the organisational puzzle need to be aligned before anything significant can be achieved. In that case, you may not be learning what it takes to influence at a strategic level.

- You may not be getting the chance to progress, perhaps because your presence inside the cordon has become too important to let you go.

These are clearly cases where that protection is not working in your best interests. Staying connected outside the cordon will help, but if you're also experiencing these side effects you will need to be much more proactive in managing your own career and personal development.

What can work well is to be quite specific about what you want to do and why and then to ask for it directly. Say something like:

- *'I need to gain more experience in X and so would like to e.g. [go to the monthly Risk Assessment meeting].'*

- Or be even more assertive: *'I want to see how Y works, as it's an area I might be interested in in the future. I'm going to approach [person] and ask if I can help out with Y occasionally.'*

Most Martyrs will not deny and may even actively help with these kinds of requests because, on principle, they do care about you and your career.

Don't be a Martyr yourself

Occasionally there's some fall-out from being closely associated with a Martyr. This can happen if they disconnect too far from the rest of the organisation and then fail to make progress on a crucial project. At those times, if they've struggled to deal with the situation, businesses may decide to just restructure the problem away.

If you've followed the tactics here, you will already have some idea when or if this kind of restructuring is about to happen and will have been proactively managing your own career. To limit any further negative impact on you, think carefully about when to jump ship, when to seek help from allies outside the department and when to take a timely step back from things.

Never be afraid, embarrassed or too loyal to prioritise your own career and work–life balance.

Growth tips for Martyrs

Here are the most useful topics to cover if you're a leader-mentor, a coach or a human resources professional who wants to help develop a Martyr.

Note that you might experience some resistance, perhaps around them being too busy to show up for a coaching session, or paying lip service to suggestions from human resources colleagues. If this happens you can use the tips for leaders described previously (see Revealing your own principles) to help gain rapport and trust.

Explore how they see others

Martyrs have a tendency to regard other people as weak, timid, uncommitted, uncaring and lacking integrity. This applies especially to people in authority who they feel are not working flat-out with them towards an uncompromising solution. And to their own teams, who they often feel need protecting.

It's worth exploring these negative judgements in some depth because they reflect a limiting perspective that will hinder progress towards the goal that your Martyr really cares about. Ask them to reflect on these questions:

- What's actually true about those judgements – and what isn't?

- What's the benefit to your Martyr of holding those judgements? That is, what does it give them a reason to do? Or, what kind of behaviours on their part do these judgements provide an excuse for? What does it enable them to feel about themselves?

- What barriers are put in place by holding these kinds of judgements? What do they make harder and what do they put out of reach?

- What would a slightly less judgemental view of those stakeholders or other people in authority make possible? And what could that lead to?

Explore barriers to compromise

A Martyr might not be aware of what seems, to others at least, like a problematic refusal to compromise. And yet compromise can often be the door that opens the way to genuine progress. Again guide them through some fairly open exploration, perhaps covering:

- Are there any fears or concerns about being blamed or held accountable for a less-than-perfect solution if they were to compromise? What about any fears or concerns about the impact that compromise might have on other people, especially end users or team members?

- How could a person who is highly principled also find it possible to make compromises for the sake of the greater good? What would that take? And what would it make possible?

- What might have to be compromised in order for progress to be made? And what could help make that acceptable?

Develop strategic influencing skills

The Martyrs I've coached have been reluctant to do strategic influencing. They don't naturally look at the big picture of who needs to be influenced so that they can achieve their goals. They don't like to be 'manipulative' in this way and believe that people should just 'get' that the thing you're working on is worth supporting wholeheartedly.

Their strategic influencing development is about both the who – *who* needs to be influenced and the what – *what* can be safely traded with those people so that we still get a good-enough solution. There are some coaching techniques that have helped:

- Stakeholder mapping for the *who*; and

- Process-mapping or project-planning tools for the *what*.

But I think that the most helpful thing, as far as possible, is to ask your Martyr to connect with their stakeholders on a more personal level. Once they see them as individual people and not distant frustrations, it becomes easier for them to find ways to address those people's needs and concerns as well.

Shift the beliefs that lead to self-sacrifice

If I could put the Martyr's tendency to self-sacrifice at work into words that encapsulate their inner beliefs, it would go something like this:

'What I'm doing is really important. "They" (a distant authority) are not entirely behind me, so I'm going to have to do it anyway. The people around me aren't as strong as me, so I'm going to have to do a lot of it by myself. And I can't afford to fail because then I wouldn't be the kind of person who makes it work despite everything.'

This belief is a powerful driver and can lead them to make great sacrifices in their health, work–life balance, relationships and long-term goals.

The most important next step for their development is to help them raise awareness of any self-sacrificing pattern. Once it's out in the light, then they can begin to make more rounded and informed choices about whether that's what they really want.

Here are some points that could be included:

- What are the warning signs that they might be self-sacrificing, perhaps in terms of their health and work–life balance?
- What's the cost of always working against or in spite of opposition?
- What else is also so important to them that they might be prepared to *stop* self-sacrificing?

Summary

- -

There's often a great sense of relief when a potential Martyr arrives to deal with a large, complex objective. Here at last, you might feel, is someone who will not rest until our goal is accomplished.

I think it's very tempting for organisations to buy into this vision of the Martyr holding up a torch as they lead their gallant followers into a critical battle. Part of that temptation is for boards and management teams to put aside any lingering concerns that the objective as it currently stands might be unachievable. It's tempting for Martyrs too, because their great strengths of principle, work ethic and the loyalty they inspire will have previously overcome a lot of similarly demanding situations.

But when there's a complex objective that might require a compromise solution, an authority group that hasn't quite been as engaged as it should, and a workforce that needs some care and development, then we're likely to be facing a difficult person situation.

For leaders of Martyrs, it's crucial to re-engage with them around their principles. They need coaching on why it's important to influence stakeholders and where to compromise for the sake of progress on the bigger agenda. Leaders can help them to deal with unconscious fears around the culture of failure in their organisation. And they can support a Martyr in avoiding the dangers of self-sacrifice, which serves nobody in the long run.

Colleagues of a Martyr can sometimes find themselves being criticised and judged for not living up to the standards this person sets – and will want to redefine a healthy boundary around it. At other times, they may need to break through the Martyr's defensive cordon, so that their own work priorities don't suffer. Similarly, a Martyr's team members might find they need to break *out* of that cordon, so that their own connections, development and even their careers aren't sacrificed to the cause.

The development process for a Martyr requires building trust in yourself as a principled person. With that trust, you can then coach them to explore what's behind the negative judgements they might be making about others. You can work on why and how to compromise for the sake of the greater good and on who and what is involved when influencing is needed to make progress. And you can also examine the unhelpful beliefs that might be leading them to self-sacrifice.

With the approach described in this chapter, a Martyr at work can become someone seriously committed to going the extra mile, able to influence away any roadblocks, supported by passionate followers and sustained by their own healthy work–life balance.

In the next chapter, we'll consider the most head-on of the difficult people at work, someone whose love for a challenge can itself be challenging to deal with – the Driving Force.

Note

1 Tzu, Lao (n.d.), as cited in 'When I let go of what I am, I become what I might be', Philosiblog. 19 July 2012. Last accessed 22 June 2023.

chapter 13

———

Type 4 – The Driving Force

'Unhappy is the land that needs a hero.'

Bertold Brecht[1]

In a nutshell

The Driving Force is usually a very resourceful, decisive and can-do person. They believe in their ability to overcome obstacles and, if necessary, to learn how to do so as they go.

Key characteristics: This person is likely to be a leader, perhaps heading up a large department or running a small independent consultancy. They love to rise to a challenge.

Why others can find them difficult: Issues at work tend to arise because of their low tolerance for colleagues who won't also meet every challenge head on; when they become impatient with the 'timid' corporate agenda; and when they have bitten off more than they can chew and need to retrench rapidly.

Example

Kam has always been picked as a leader, whether as captain of the school team or director of the new division. Others find his self-belief and willingness to take on a challenge just unstoppable. He doesn't have time for people without self-confidence and can be fiercely critical. He's had his hands burned more than once taking on so much, but worries that if he doesn't he'll run out of time to fulfil his potential.

At their best

The Driving force is capable of heroic levels of achievement, moving mountains to get things done. They have often discovered how to be so resourceful by themselves and therefore believe that they will be able to learn or acquire whatever is needed to achieve their goals. As a leader, they actively seek out team members who have a similar can-do attitude, prizing those qualities above ability and experience. If they have also learned how to influence, rely on and value colleagues with very different attitudes to theirs, they can be brilliantly unstoppable.

When do things get difficult?

First, the Driving Force often has a low tolerance for others who don't automatically roll up their sleeves in anticipation of a significant problem or opportunity. At which point they may become overbearing; trampling over other people's agendas and ramping up the pressure on them to comply, with little regard for the interpersonal fall-out.

Second, their tendency to seek out challenges may also cause them to ignore established corporate priorities and become extremely frustrated and outspoken critics of what they see as a 'timid' agenda. This further reduces their ability to make progress or to shape the wider agenda.

Third, a Driving Force has such high levels of belief in their ability to get stuff done that they can develop a pattern of taking on more and more until it's suddenly too much even for them to cope with, forcing a rapid retrenchment.

Their place in the Matrix of Difficult People

	T	S	P
D	😏	🤯	😇
E	😠	🙂	😎
A	😬	😑	😳

Attention Focus

Task focused – the Driving Force's primary focus, and the lens through which they will assess progress and set priorities, is on discrete tasks or projects that have tangible outcomes.

Stress Strategy

Excess – under pressure, the Driving Force will ramp up their energy, bringing as much weight to bear as they can on whatever they feel is standing in the way.

How to spot a Driving Force

'Like getting hit by a truck'

One chief executive had this rueful warning about working with a Driving Force who had become difficult, *'If you try to stand in their way, it's like getting hit by a truck.'*

Look out for someone who simply will not be argued or disagreed with and who will bear down on you with tremendous force if you try. If they've become really difficult, you may discover that they keep digging in, deeper and deeper, or that they deliver threats or ultimatums.

Disregard for the 'weaklings'

Even a Driving Force who has become difficult at work *will* collaborate and compromise. It's *who* they will listen to and take notice of that can cause problems.

They may not be open to differing views and approaches from people that they perceive as lacking in personal power. This means they may disregard anyone who does not seem to share their own driving qualities, regardless of the actual authority that person holds. This can cause a lot of friction and set some powerful people against them.

Impatience with the corporate agenda

Once you've approved a strategy – for example, you've identified a threat or spotted an opportunity and have agreed on what needs to be done – you may find that a Driving Force will want to immediately throw everything at it. And they may try to do this despite whatever pace and sequence you've already agreed on. Others can find this unrealistic and overwhelming, and be unsettled by it.

Tips for leaders of a Driving Force

Leaders who manage to win the respect of a Driving Force and help them to get comfortable with the corporateness, politicking and diversity of organisational life will discover that they have a valuable, loyal and brilliantly unstoppable team member.

For leaders, the key thing is to utilise a Driving Force's own strengths. They believe that they can develop or acquire everything that's needed to achieve their goals – so use that belief.

Developing mutual respect

A Driving Force values directness and resourcefulness. To win their respect they will need to understand *your* version of these qualities. And you can be direct in this too. Look for opportunities to talk directly about your strategy, in particular:

- Why are you doing things the way you do – what's the **outcome** you're shooting for?

Similarly watch out for times when you might be unconsciously judged by a Driving Force for being less than resourceful. When might your approach appear lazy, weak or too indirect? Talk with them about why you have adopted this approach – again, what outcome does it lead to?

Finally, in terms of developing mutual respect, what happens if your own natural leadership style is also very can-do and challenge-ready? Are you clashing with a Driving Force because you share some of those qualities? If that's the case, the answer is to:

- Make sure you're not being excessively forceful because you're under stress and you worry that something important may not otherwise happen.
- Make sure you're being flexible in balancing the tasks/systems/ people focus of your own attention (see Chapter 5).

Agenda alignment

Leaders might not realise that they need to be quite proactive and even directive in making sure that their Driving Force's agenda is aligned with that of the organisation.

All of the Driving Forces I've worked with want to fully use their capabilities. Because of this, they will often be frustrated at what they see as organisational timidity. They'll be wondering why others don't seem to share their determination to get on and do what's been agreed.

But their impatience may cause them to ignore the agreed corporate priorities that help to direct the efforts of the whole organisation, not just their part of it. They can become an unhelpfully outspoken critic or a real loose cannon. To deal with this, leaders should draw them into a closer alliance, using a two-pronged approach.

First, be prepared to share information about the corporate agenda that you might not routinely talk about. Especially:

- At your level and above, what is the consensus about the priority tasks that need to be tackled across the business?
- What tasks are *not* seen as a priority by people at that level right now?

Second, of those priorities, what do you and your own bosses and colleagues see as being the most important contribution your Driving Force should be making?

I think they just need to know that the organisation is aware of the priorities and isn't running scared from them. Once you've done that, your objective is to come to a mutual understanding about how their strengths can best be used in a way that aligns with what the business actually needs.

Acquisition of new soft skills

A Driving Force who is being experienced by others as a difficult person is actually relatively easy to develop out of it – if you can get to them before they become overstretched or decide to head off into the horizon looking for more worthy challenges.

Previously they will have traded on their ability to get things done despite the obstacles. They'll probably agree with the phrase, *'You can't make an omelette without breaking eggs.'* If they've now got to the point where this pattern is causing difficulties for other people, then it's probably time for them to acquire some new capabilities. Again, be direct in this, perhaps even demanding about it. I've set out the most important soft skills areas at the end of this chapter in the section on growth tips. From a leadership point of view, you might want to emphasise those on:

- Making their efforts sustainable, so that they don't repeat any patterns around getting overstretched and then having to retrench
- Being able to value and influence a much wider range of people, not just those who share their can-do approach.

Career planning

Balance and overload are tricky issues when it comes to a Driving Force. They usually do fine taking on more and more challenges – right up to the point where it tips over into being too much. Part of why they do this is just habit; overusing a strength. But part of it is also a concern that they'll run out of time in their career and never get to the point where they're using all of their capability.

Opportunities to demonstrate that capability are often what catch out a Driving Force and tip them into overload. They need to prioritise and sequence those opportunities instead of trying to grab them all in parallel.

Leaders can encourage them to develop a simple career plan so that they feel less pressure to achieve everything right away and can see that such opportunities do come around more than once. Help them to build a wide and solid foundation from which to make the most of such opportunities. In the long run that's much better than anxiously aiming to moon-shot all of them.

Tips for colleagues and staff of a Driving Force

From the Driving Force's point of view, there are perhaps only three categories of acceptable behaviour at work – lead, follow or get out of the way!

Your experience of working alongside a Driving Force will very much depend on which category they (and perhaps you yourself) feel you fit into. Use the suggested tactics below in the light of that knowledge and pick those that seem most useful to you and your circumstances.

Find the win-wins not the win-loses

As the colleague of a Driving Force you may find yourself at odds with them if:

1 You're not prepared to acquiesce to something the Driving Force wants to do; or

2 You're trying to make progress on a project that would cut across something the Driving Force is working on.

You may find that your Driving Force is being quite combative about this, trying to win (and thus have you lose) rather than looking for ways to co-operate.

You'll need to be pretty assertive about this. Make sure that you have the backing of key allies and then be prepared to stand your ground. Win-lose is a really sub-optimal approach within an organisation and the Driving Force needs to be told this, directly.

In parallel, consider what you might offer that would enable a win-win situation:

- What could you both stand to gain, if a win-win could be found?
- What co-operation would you be prepared to offer?
- What's the minimum level of support you'd need in return?

Workload boundaries

A Driving Force might expect you to be onboard and working with a force at least similar to theirs, on everything they're juggling. Which can be a lot.

But working at an unacceptable and unsustainable pace or level is a boundary issue and you must act if a Driving Force isn't respecting your limits. In that case, the best chance of a good outcome is to take the following approach:

1 Be direct and specific in saying what's happening.

2 Don't prevaricate, don't be subtle, don't be vague.

3 Offer a solution rather than just stating the problem.

It's best to say something like:

- *'I'm working too hard/too fast and it doesn't feel sustainable. I need to slow down/row back on task X so I can continue to contribute properly. I believe the way to do that is [offer a solution].'*

And you could also try something like this, by referring to an established benchmark:

- *'I think the expectations of what I should be achieving are out of line with what's required elsewhere in the organisation. I want to be part of what we're doing here. And to be able to keep doing that I need to prioritise and not juggle so much at once. Here are the things I feel should be top priorities and here are the things I'm going to need to slow down on for a while: [offer a solution].'*

The 'Just Do It' way to influence a Driving Force

A Driving Force can also sometimes be bad at taking into account the views and approaches of people who don't share their traits.

If you do need to influence a Driving Force, or you notice that they're not valuing what you say or how you do things, here's how to tackle it:

- Always talk or present to them in terms of positive outcomes. For example: *'By doing this, we can achieve X.'* Or, *'If we include [this idea], we can gain a real advantage over Y.'*

- Talk and behave in a proactive way. For example: *'I just jumped in and got on with this, so that we could make some progress.'* Or, *'If we don't wait and we just get on with it, now is a good time to get a head start.'*

- Try not to seem too prescriptive in the way that things have to be done. Driving Forces tend to be good seat-of-the-pants pilots, preferring to figure out the *how* as they go. Don't say: *'We need to start with X and then do Y and then make sure we don't do Z.'*

- Do say things like: *'There's a couple of key points we'll need to hit along the way and some hard limits we'll want to navigate around. Let's list those, so that we don't forget them, and then we can just get on with it.'*

Take charge of your own development

Because they'll probably have learned for themselves how to be so resourceful, a Driving Force can forget that other people might need a more structured and long-term approach to their learning and development. Or that others might not have quite so much confidence in their ability to acquire new skills or move on in their careers and may need to take it slower and be more methodical.

Your Driving Force may be expecting you to take charge of your own development, as they usually do for themselves.

Again, the best tactic is to:

- Be proactive – make sure you do develop a career and learning and development plan.
- Be direct – ask for what you need and say what support you will want from them.
- Be assertive – stand your ground against any counter-suggestions that don't suit your plans: *'This is what I need to learn because this is where I want to get to.'*

Be wary that your Driving Force may try to ramp up your development plans, encouraging you to aim higher or go faster. That's fine, as long as it's what you really want and will suit your style. Driving Forces are bad at knowing when they themselves are about to get overloaded and may not be aware of what will overload you.

Growth tips for Driving Forces

Anybody who is helping a Driving Force with their own development – an HR colleague, a leader-mentor or a coach – might be tempted to harness their force so that they take charge of their own development and push through any useful changes themselves.

But this is a good leadership tactic, and less so a good developmental approach. The Driving Force has probably *always* approached their own development in that self-determined way. To have reached the point where others are finding them difficult is a clear sign that a different approach is now needed. An approach that also gets to the heart of what drives them and asks, 'When is enough, enough?' before doing anything else. That's why my approach usually starts with the mindset shifts below.

Mindset shifts

It's definitely worth exploring what it is that pushes a Driving Force onwards and upwards with such determination. There are two areas of mindset shifts to prioritise:

First, how they really feel about themselves. As boldly and compassionately as possible, help them to explore the following:

- Might they be measuring their self-worth mostly or solely on the basis of what they can achieve at work?

- What is the cost of that kind of measure – perhaps in terms of its impact on their peace of mind and the people closest to them outside of work?

- What other ways of measuring contribution or achievement might be *more* useful to them?

- What would it make possible, if they didn't need to do or achieve *anything*, in order to be worthy or of value in the world?

Second, explore their experiences of being powerless or without resources. Or of having to really struggle, just to stay afloat. There's usually a reason why people have learned to be as resourceful as a typical Driving Force – and it's often been out of necessity.

Once learned, it's a hard lesson to put aside and it explains why some Driving Forces always seem to adopt that *Excess* stress strategy, striving harder and harder. Even when it just makes things worse or leads to overload. Explore the following with them:

- What if they needed that ability to be so resourceful at some previous point in their lives and work, but that it has now served its purpose?

- What if, now, the ability to rise to every challenge is just one possible tool in their toolbox and doesn't have to be the *only* one they use?

- What could that realisation lead to or make possible?

Making effort sustainable

The partner to exploring those mindset shifts is for Driving Forces to develop a habit of consciously checking how sustainable their efforts are. Even if they aren't ready to tackle the underlying causes, they can still just use this as a tool or check-step.

There are two easy points for them to consider:

- Pareto's Law – that the first 20 per cent of one's effort often achieves 80 per cent of the results. And that the final 20 per cent of the results may take *another* 80 per cent of one's effort. They need to spot those times when 80 per cent is good enough.

- That successful people at work usually hold back some energy to apply in building relationships and in keeping themselves fresh. Without the headroom of a reserve of energy, a Driving Force has much less scope for getting on with others and adapting their behaviours.

And one slightly harder point for them to consider is that, unlike other types, a Driving Force's overload point is more like a sudden cliff edge than a steep mountain climb.

Take them back to some instances in the past just before they got overloaded.

What did it feel like back then? They'll probably tell you it was like surfing a wave. Or they'll talk about how alive they felt or how everything seemed easy, that time almost slowed down. This is what athletes often call 'being in the zone' and it's a sign of being stretched to peak performance.

They need to know that when they experience that sense of being in the zone – *that is almost certainly when they have also reached their maximum load*. And that is the time to *not* take on anything else, even though everything feels easy, like surfing, at that point.

Valuing and influencing others

An important part of the learning and development for a Driving Force is to discover how they can value other people for who they are, and for their differences, rather than whether or not they share a can-do trait.

Without learning this, a Driving Force will always find that there are limits on how they relate to the wider circle of their colleagues and bosses and limits to how much they can influence the course of events in their organisation. There are three parts to this:

- Use curiosity about what makes other people tick. It's possible to discover other people's values by observing the choices they make, how things make them feel, what they prioritise and what they react against.

- Take a functional view about what someone else's style of thinking and behaving makes possible – for them and for the others around them. What are the genuine benefits of behaving the way that this other person behaves?

- Look for compromises and win-wins. An important part of growth for a Driving Force is learning to cede some control so that others can also get what they want. Finding those mutual win-wins will seriously boost their ability to influence the bigger agenda at work.

Summary

I've enjoyed working with Driving Forces, both as their leader and as their coach.

As their leader it was sometimes a little scary at first, to experience all that energy and force, which could feel like it was directed at me when I wasn't prepared to get out of the way. Harnessing that energy was straightforward (although I often had to do some relationship-repairing in their wake). It was about establishing – maybe even demanding – mutual respect and looking for ways to help align their agenda to that of the organisation.

What was less easy as a leader was getting them to shift their style a little, so that they could thrive in different circumstances, with other powerful stakeholders. It wasn't until I had some coaching tools under my belt that those kinds of shifts became easier to facilitate. I also experienced how a Driving Force can suddenly tip over into overload, to go from riding the wave to being submerged by it. This is a vital watchpoint for their leaders.

As a colleague or team member of a Driving Force, there's a lot of boundary-establishing and protecting to do. This applies to your behavioural approach and how assertively you insist on looking for win-wins; with your own workload boundaries, and with making sure that your own development needs are supported. Fortunately, a Driving Force is likely to respond well to a direct, proactive and outcome-focused representation and so will be relatively easy to influence, once you make the attempt.

The development needs for a Driving Force are about understanding what's underneath that drive, so that they can develop more choice and flexibility in when and how it's applied. Similarly, helping them to become more conscious of what it feels like to be surfing their peak performance wave will help them to create new patterns of more sustainable effort and avoid sudden overload. Those developments make possible the crucial next step for a Driving Force who is being experienced as difficult at work – their influencing.

When you have a Driving Force in your business who has also learned how to influence, rely on and value colleagues with different attitudes, then they really are unstoppable. At that point, you've got someone who has become much less like a bulldozer and much more of a bridge builder. Someone who can take all kinds of people with them and really get stuff done.

In the next chapter we'll meet another difficult person, someone who can make you feel like you've got hold of a tiger by its tail – the Revolutionary.

Note

1 Brecht, Bertolt, 'A life of Galileo', in *Modern Plays*, edited by Mark Ravenhill, Bloomsbury Methuen Drama 2013.

chapter 14

Type 5 – The Revolutionary

'Passion is needed for any great work, and for the revolution, passion and audacity are required in big doses.'

Che Guevara[1]

In a nutshell

The Revolutionary is usually a self-starting, enthusiastic person who is great at finding out about new ideas and different approaches.

Key characteristics: This person readily embraces change and will push for fast and wide-ranging transformation regardless of its wider implications.

Why others can find them difficult: Issues at work can arise from their desire to change everything as far and as fast as possible, often acting without consensus or regard for fallout.

Example

Simone jumped at the opportunity when the board asked her to lead a long-overdue change programme. Her passion helped to recruit keen like-minded supporters and they quickly got going on a lot of fronts. But before long, senior figures began complaining that things were happening too fast, without proper discussion. Simone pressed on, introducing new ideas and working ever harder, trying to stop progress from stalling.

At their best

They are an outspoken champion for how much better things could be. As a leader they have an infectious and impatient energy and a well-developed ability to seek out different ways of doing things and adapt them to suit their organisation. They won't rest until the far-reaching transformations they envisage are complete. They will seek out and promote allies and are prepared to courageously lead them from the front.

When do things get difficult?

The Revolutionary feels the need for change. When there is consensus, and the right forces are aligned, they are tireless and charismatic proponents for improvement. But in the wrong situations there are three areas where they can find themselves being called difficult.

First, they may readily exceed the boundaries of what's expected of them and find it hard to know where to stop. In their view as soon as you consider changing one thing it becomes apparent what else needs changing, regardless of whether or not that is in their remit.

Second, they can often enjoy and maintain an incredible pace of work, since they find it so compelling. However, they and others around them are at risk of burnout. Even potential allies can find the scope and pace of change quite overwhelming, in which case they may reduce their support, fall by the wayside or even become an opponent.

Third, the Revolutionary's ability to adopt and synthesise ideas and approaches is very well developed. As a consequence they can sometimes overlook the slow, iterative political consensus-building that other people may need before being ready to adopt new ideas and new ways of working themselves.

Their place in the Matrix of Difficult People

	T	S	P
D			
E			
A			

Attention Focus

Systems focused – the Revolutionary's primary focus, and the lens through which they assess things, is on interconnected systems and how those mesh together.

Stress Strategy

Excess – under pressure the Revolutionary will tend to ramp up their own effort and energy, bringing more force to bear on their rationale for and the scope of change.

How to spot a Revolutionary

Holding a tiger by the tail

Working with a Revolutionary may feel a bit like holding a tiger by the tail. Things are relatively safe as long as you don't even think about letting go. But of course, the tiger doesn't want to be held and will make that pretty clear!

Burnout by association

As a colleague or team member of a Revolutionary, you may notice how tiring it is. First, there's the need to understand how everything joins up. Then there's the constant identification of new people, ideas and resources that will help. And then there's the sheer pace of it all.

Fallout

You may notice the political or social fallout caused by a Revolutionary's actions. Faced with the slow pace of understanding and consensus-building, or simply non-comprehension of possible opposing viewpoints, the Revolutionary may have charged ahead anyway and metaphorically derailed a train or blown up a carefully constructed organisational bridge.

Tips for leaders of a Revolutionary

Leading a Revolutionary is not a place for the indecisive or faint-hearted! If you can help them to navigate the wider political environment, guide and shape the focus of their efforts, and help to keep the pace of change sustainable, then you'll have a powerful change agent on your team. I've set out some more details on each of those in the tips below.

Check that they're the right person

Above all, it seems to me that part of the role of leading a Revolutionary is to make sure that you've got the right person in the right place at the right time. You could ask yourself:

- Is the change that they passionately want to enact actually what is needed?
- Should that change be delivered in a revolutionary way – fast, extensive, loud and visible?
- Are you ready and able to deal with the consequences?

You can't really put a lid on your Revolutionary, at least not without either totally wasting or potentially damaging them. If you've answered 'No' to the questions above, then you have a square peg in a round hole and need to deal with that. But if you've generally answered 'Yes', then here are some more tips for leading a Revolutionary in a way that might just work for everybody.

Define your common ground

Your Revolutionary will be unconsciously testing your own commitment, constantly asking themselves, 'Is my boss aligned with what needs to happen?' Connect your own motivation with the cause that you've employed this person to tackle. This is where the two of you will find your common ground:

- What are you asking them to do?
- Why is that important – both in general and specifically to you?
- How well are you able to express your own devotion to the cause?

In finding your common ground, it's important to put a limit on things, to define the edges of that ground. Consider these questions:

- Where are the absolute boundaries of what you're trying to achieve – and therefore what should they *not* go beyond?
- What must *not* happen?
- What bridges must *not* be burned?

You effectively need to say to them something like: *'In service of our common goal, here's where I would really appreciate your directing the majority of your efforts. How can I best help with that?'* And be prepared to do this a lot.

Being a Revolutionary can be a lonely thing – imagine them up there in the hills, behind enemy lines, cut off from fresh resources, not knowing what's going on back at base. Your leadership is vital in keeping their efforts directed at the right common ground.

Snowplough leadership

When you're leading a Revolutionary, Snowplough leadership is a great way to remind yourself that you'll need to be watching and clearing the road for them – and dealing with any fallout. It's probably time to grab your shovel!

Here are some key things to consider. If you can, run through this checklist jointly with your Revolutionary:

- What doors can you open for them? Particularly to other people who might welcome your own, perhaps less upfront, interpersonal style.

- Where do you need to be smoothing out the political pathway? For example, who might be a useful ally if you bring them around to the cause? Who might disagree with or block the agenda, unless you help to persuade them otherwise?

- How might you visibly and publicly show your support for the common ground agenda?

- What fallout do you need to be prepared to deal with?

- Where else can you help your Revolutionary to gain traction on what might otherwise be slippery territory?

Anti-burnout pastoral care

Your Revolutionary is likely to be treading a fine line between spearheading the revolution and burning themselves out – and possibly taking others down with them. Leaders will probably need to actively step in and check what's happening.

As well as filling in for something that a Revolutionary tends not to do, you can role model the importance of this to them. It's a job that individuals should be doing for themselves (however devoted to the cause they might be) and an oversight responsibility that leaders should be taking on for their people.

Find out if pastoral care measures are being put to use, such as:

- Are they taking breaks and holidays?
- What practical issues are being a drain on their physical, emotional and mental reserves?
- When's their downtime from the responsibility of putting the world to rights?
- What recharges their batteries – and when do they do this?
- How close are they to having bitten off too much to chew – and how would they know?
- Are they running a similar checklist to make sure that their own teams and the key people around them are also not at risk of being burnt out?

Tips for colleagues and staff of Revolutionaries

Working for or alongside a Revolutionary is likely to be exhilarating, exasperating and exhausting – and probably all at once!

Exhilarating, because here at last is someone who is driven to change everything and to change it fast, regardless of the wider implications. Exasperating, because they feel the need to do everything at once rather than plan, prioritise and follow a process. And they can be their own worst enemy when it comes to rubbing people up the wrong way. Exhausting, because of the unrelenting pace and the assimilation of every new bit of information they uncover – each of which might cause them to change their approach.

If any of that feels familiar to you, here are some suggested tactics for thriving alongside a Revolutionary boss or colleague.

Boundary management

A Revolutionary boss or colleague can feel quite demanding of your time, attention and effort. They don't always mean to make it feel like this but they will often assume that their own revolutionary zeal should be shared by everyone else. And because their focus is on interconnected systems, rather than people or tasks, they won't always notice *who* is being impacted or just *how many* tasks are piling up.

Therefore, it will be partly down to you to make it explicitly clear:

1 What you're *not* prepared to do
2 That you need to work reasonable hours and have a life outside of work
3 That other things also need to get done.

It has been my experience that Revolutionaries are not usually hostile to having your boundaries pointed out to them in the way that some other Difficult People can be. More usually, it is colleagues and staff who get caught up in that zeal themselves. Colleagues are likely to go out of their way to support a Revolutionary, often because they know the consequences if they let the Revolutionary go charging off by themselves. Staff of Revolutionaries are likely to overstretch themselves, since they're following someone who sets such a fanatical example.

The key then is to be very proactive and open about which boundaries are important to you, to be aware of when you're reaching a limit and to share this information.

Planning and project management

Because a Revolutionary's attention focus is on *Systems*, they are acutely aware that everything is connected to everything else in some way. When you combine this with their *Excess* stress strategy, the end result often means (in their minds) that the change they so want to bring about necessitates a lot of change in a lot of places at once.

This makes them consummate plate-spinners and they will tend to spread their attention wide across all the potential targets.

For colleagues and staff of a Revolutionary it is critically important to counter these tendencies with some practical planning and project management. Approaches that include the task- and people focus that Revolutionaries sometimes overlook.

If you work alongside a Revolutionary, you might want to insist on having both:

1 An overall plan that describes what you are trying to achieve, how it'll be done and how you'll measure its success

2 Project-management approaches that help to establish what the *priorities* are at any given time, in which *sequence* specific tasks need to be done, and what *resources* are required.

This approach is unlikely to come naturally to your Revolutionary but in my experience they will appreciate being supported by people who can operate this way and who insist on the kind of assurance that it gives to actually delivering change.

If your boss is a Revolutionary and is reluctant to adopt a project-management approach, you may need to push back a little if they're jumping the gun or not thinking things through. These replies are designed to push responsibility back to them, so that you don't get burnt out or caught in the fallout of something:

- *'Yes, I can do Task D – AND I still need to do these specific things A, B and C, first.'*

- *'Yes, that outcome is possible to achieve – AND it will require these resources [list them] first.'*

- *'If we're now changing focus and are doing Task X, what do you want me to drop or stop doing to make that possible?'*

And don't forget your boundary management from the first tip above.

Allies and consensus

The pace and extent of the change that Revolutionaries would like to see, along with their ability to assimilate new information and change the scope to include it, can leave allies by the wayside. And the Revolutionary themselves is often reluctant to slow down and do the consensus-building that would make it easier for allies to get on board (and to keep up).

This is counterproductive and because of it they can sometimes be in opposition to a powerful status quo.

For those who work with or for a Revolutionary, it's important to make sure you don't adopt all of that tendency. The modern workplace needs Revolutionaries, but in the words of the African proverb:

> *'If you want to go fast, go alone. If you want to go far, go together.'*

Make sure you're doing three things that your Revolutionary might not do by themselves:

1 Look out for **potential allies**. Who might help you do what you're trying to do? Who might just be a sympathetic ear that you can share your troubles with?

2 Take time to **build bridges and explain things** to colleagues and other stakeholders. And don't be embarrassed over having to explain that things might all change again tomorrow if you can't convince your Revolutionary boss that their latest idea isn't on the Gantt chart.

3 **Stay safe**. Make reference to your boundaries. Refuse to do things which might blow up in your face because other powerful forces in the organisation have not been smoothed away. Especially use your allies if you're in this kind of situation.

Growth tips for Revolutionaries

Helping a Revolutionary as a coach, a leader-mentor or a human resources professional can be an inspiring experience and they are often a great source of interesting new ideas or radical approaches that you'll want to know more about. On the other hand, you may find your authenticity and commitment being judged. And there are also a couple of traps to avoid, in how you develop rapport and in making sure the experience doesn't burn you out.

Resistance to overcome

Revolutionaries often tell me that they're surprised and frustrated that others don't share their passion and urgency about what needs to change. Or of how others don't share their belief of how it is all connected, so that change needs to happen on multiple fronts simultaneously, to be of any use. Because of this, they are likely to be unconsciously testing whether or not you genuinely support their cause – and support it strongly enough. If they sense that you are not committed, they may resist any attempts to be helped.

You'll first need to take these three steps to overcome that resistance:

1 **Be open and honest about your own agenda.** Which means saying something like this: *'My agenda isn't the same as yours. I'm not here to do your job. Rather, I'm here to support and develop you, so that you can be at your best.'*

2 **Don't take sides.** Organisations sometimes appoint Revolutionaries to carry out transformative, disruptive change – but then find that they really don't like the disruption this causes. You need to be neutral and rational about this and not blaming of the organisation, otherwise you'll just enable more of that resistance. Recognise how organisations sometimes do this. It's an inconvenient fact of life. And then move the discussion on to the positive, by asking, *'So this is how it is – what's the best way to deal with this kind of situation?'*

3 **Gain rapport by authentically matching three of a Revolutionary's key patterns:**

- A high-energy determination to make a difference for them – but don't get burnt out or too swept up in things.

- Think of their development as a system – a series of interconnected things to work on. You could say to them, *'We have to work on all of these aspects of you because they all connect within who you are.'*

- When they ramp up energy, either in resistance to or in agreement with you, match it at first. Don't immediately back down in the face of it. Once you have established rapport, then you can model a slightly less always-intense approach.

Mindset shifts

In common with several of the other types of Difficult People, it's sometimes hard to spot that Revolutionaries have self-doubt (and other limiting ways of thinking) because these are often masked by their readiness to embrace change and push for transformation. It's worth exploring three types of mindset issues with your Revolutionary, because these are what will be pushing them further into their *Excess* stress response. Help them to shift these, and they'll have more choice about how they respond when they're under pressure and outside their comfort zone:

- **Self-doubt** – do they have any unstated doubts about their ability to plan and organise? Or doubts about how well they can build alliances or connect with people who don't think like they do? Get any such doubts out in the open. That's often 80 per cent of the solution, and then you can work on finding a way around those doubts.

- **Shame** – Revolutionaries are sometimes driven to make a massive difference in their work because they unconsciously don't believe that they are a 'good enough' person. Again, just helping them to be more conscious of this as a driver of their behaviour can often create a big shift.

- **Guessing** – for Revolutionaries, who tend to work best behind the lines, guessing at what others are thinking and at what their agenda is can get in the way of building consensus and creating allies. Ask what they really know about other people's agendas. Who have they really talked to, in depth? Are they aware that they might just be guessing at what others think?

Skills to develop

The Matrix of Difficult People helps to identify what kinds of skills and abilities Revolutionaries might benefit from developing further. Their attention focus is on *Systems*, so they may not have highly developed skills in the other two columns of the matrix, including:

- **Task-focused skills**, such as project management, planning and scope definition. They may instead have relied on their energy and drive to just soak up tasks rather than manage them effectively.

- **People-focused skills**, such as influencing, alliance-building and consensus-building. They may have previously relied on their zeal to attract like-minded supporters but unintentionally set themselves in opposition to people who don't immediately share their agenda.

Healthy boundaries and other support

Revolutionaries do have a tendency to define themselves by their work. That's not necessarily a bad thing, so long as it's not causing them to burn out. Explore what a set of healthy and sustainable boundaries might look like for them.

In addition, the way Revolutionaries go all out for change can lead to conflict with others. But too much conflict is itself stressful and having mutually supportive relationships is one of the key ways of keeping ourselves going when the going gets tough. The influencing skills described here will help. You can also assist them by:

- Considering who else might be a good source of moral support, apart from their loyal followers.

- Checking that conflict hasn't become a default setting. Not everybody needs to be a zealous supporter and it's sometimes healthy to spend time around people who really aren't all that bothered about your cause.

Summary

- -

I started this chapter with a quote from the archetypal revolutionary himself – Che Guevara. A complex figure whose story tends to polarise opinions, Guevara was moved to bring about deep political and social change by the poverty, hunger and disease he witnessed as a young man. He was also accused of being an authoritarian, of seeking to impose change, sometimes violently, when faced with an entrenched opposition.

In the workplace, Revolutionaries can be outspoken champions for how much better things could be. They will seek out new and different ways of doing things. They will use their infectious and impatient energy to attract like-minded followers. And they will courageously lead them from the front, not resting until the transformations they have envisioned are complete.

In the wrong situations, they may also blindly or wilfully exceed the boundaries that have been set. And they often set such a blistering pace for change and exhibit such a mind-blowing ability to assimilate new ideas that colleagues, bosses and potential allies can be overwhelmed, burnt out or left by the wayside. They are also tempted to overlook the slow, iterative consensus-building that other people often need, perhaps becoming somewhat authoritarian in approach themselves as a result. When these things happen, they join the ranks of Difficult People at work.

Leading a Revolutionary is about making sure you've got the right person in place and that you actually want them to tackle the kind of unpopular, complex change in a way that needs radical thinking and high energy levels to deliver. In this case, you'll need to find your own common ground with them, to clear the way for them and to help make sure that they and the people around them don't get burnt out in the process.

Working alongside a Revolutionary successfully is, above all else, about setting and maintaining your own boundaries. They are usually not hostile to this, rather, just unaware that it's an option. You may also need to insist on good planning and project-management approaches, making sure that the detailed tasks and the resources required are also part of the consideration. Lastly, make sure you're not dragged into a totally 'guerrilla', them-versus-us mindset, helping instead to maintain links to allies and to the rest of the organisation.

For those human resources specialists, coaches and mentor-leaders who want to help with the professional development of a Revolutionary, you'll first need to overcome their resistance to your own authenticity. You can help them to uncover limiting self-doubts about their ability to be anything other than revolutionary in approach. You can also support them to develop the small political and influencing skills that help to get things done at work without always having to blow things up. Lastly, you can assist them in exploring what their own healthy boundaries might look like.

With the steps set out in this chapter, a Revolutionary at work can become a truly transformational leader. They can use their ability to assimilate new ideas and their desire to champion change as a way of inspiring everybody – even those who might at first disagree with them. And they can apply their energies in a targeted, effective and sustainable way, bringing about important change with the backing and support of those who matter.

In the next chapter, we'll meet a related type of person, someone who becomes difficult at work as they try to sweep up more and more control – the Empire Builder.

Note

1 Guevara, Che (n.d.), as cited in Cheguevara.org. Last accessed 22 June 2023.

chapter 15

Type 6 – The Empire Builder

'If I only had humility,
I'd be perfect.'

Ted Turner[1]

> ## In a nutshell
>
> **The Empire Builder** is usually a charismatic and visionary person with a powerful ability to recruit people to their cause.
>
> **Key characteristics:** They have a strong self-belief, rely on their supporters to handle the details and often come to the fore as leaders in times of uncertainty or challenge.
>
> **Why others can find them difficult:** Issues at work can arise from their tendency to sweep up more and more control, regardless of whether that is the best thing to do overall, from their intolerance of criticism, and from their disregard for inconvenient complications.

Example

Ibby is a popular leader in everything he does and has a real talent for saying what needs to be done in a straightforward way. People are drawn to his self-belief and like how he makes them feel valued by relying on their strengths. He prefers to be moving forwards all the time and he can't stand having to stop and mess around with complex details or being held up by those who don't agree with the direction.

At their best

Empire Builders are capable of motivating people in individual departments and even whole organisations in directions that others would find hard to galvanise. They set out a compelling vision for how things might be and make sure that the right colleagues are in place to understand the details. They've learned to be humble and open to alternative points of view, balancing the useful maverick side of their nature with a collegiate and joined-up leadership style.

When do things get difficult?

Empire Builders are energised by having people on their side, in pursuit of something that will gain them respect.

When the thing they are pursuing to win acclaim is aligned with the needs of the organisation, and there are no dissenting voices or complex stumbling blocks in the way, then they can lead substantial progress. But if those factors aren't all lined up then their progress can turn out to be fragile.

Because their focus is on who is following them, rather than on what needs to be done or on whether it all joins up, there can sometimes be serious flaws in the direction and execution of the course they are taking. They may react very badly if this is brought to their attention – shooting the messenger rather than admitting to being less than perfect.

Left unchecked, an Empire Builder might start to:

- Rid themselves of their critics – people who point out problems that would slow progress or change direction if addressed; and

- Seek more and more control and compliance in an attempt to squash dissent and continue progress.

Both of these can be self-defeating, as the people who might deal with the tricky parts of executing the strategy, or who could find workable compromises in the strategy itself, become excluded.

Their place in the Matrix of Difficult People

	T	S	P
D	😐	🤯	😇
E	😠	🙃	😎
A	😬	😑	😳

Attention Focus

People focused – the Empire Builder's primary focus is on people: their thoughts, feelings and social needs. They will assess a project partly in terms of how much acclaim and how many followers they might garner.

Stress Strategy

Excess – under pressure the Empire Builder will tend to ramp up their energy and extend their scope, seeking more compliance to exclude criticism and control progress.

How to spot an Empire Builder

'You're either for me or against me'

An Empire Builder who has become difficult at work and is having an *Excess* stress response is likely to be very clued in to who is unquestioningly following their lead and who isn't. Any criticism of their approach, or even just the pointing out of obstacles, problems or flaws in the vision that aren't easily resolved, is unlikely to be welcomed. Instead, this may be viewed as personal criticism of them and taken as evidence that you are not to be trusted as a supportive follower.

'My team can take care of that'

As the leader or colleague of an Empire Builder, you might notice them offering to handle anything and everything. Even when it isn't something they're currently responsible for, or even qualified to do. You might hear statements like, 'My team can take care of that.' This can be a sign that they're worried about another initiative, issue or project impinging on their agenda and so feel the need to sweep it up into their control. Notice also that there's likely to be an emphasis on 'my' team, as if it is an extension of themselves.

Point-blank refusal to face problems

Empire Builders have a major strength in their ability to inspire confidence and get great performance from their teams. But the price for this can be that they feel unable to show what they see as doubt, uncertainty or prevarication. They often do experience those things but prefer to hide them. Because of this, trying to convince an Empire Builder that the glamourous course of action they've set out on isn't the best option, or that it has some problems hidden in the details, can often be met with a point-blank refusal to acknowledge. Instead, they may see it as personal criticism.

Tips for leaders of an Empire Builder

At the right times, especially when there's some stress from external threats or some big opportunities in the business environment, being the leader of an Empire Builder is like 'firework leadership' – light the touchpaper and then stand well back and watch the show!

At other times, when the strategy needs to be more joined up, when there are 'wicked' issues that need compromises and collegiate solutions, or when execution needs to be steady and precise, you'll want to take a more hands-on approach to lead your Empire Builder. Here are the most important things to focus on.

Role modelling – vulnerability and vision

This is one of the most helpful things you can do for an Empire Builder. Role model how it *is* possible to be open to doubts and concerns and to face uncertain, complex problems without appearing weak. Consistently strong leadership is perhaps more about acknowledging those things so they can be dealt with in the open than it is about just powering past them.

Behaviours you might want to role model could include the following:

- Acknowledging in the company of colleagues that there are things you don't know, are uncertain about, or might even feel overwhelmed by. And asking for help in dealing with those.

- Consulting with people who might have quite different opinions to your own about what needs to be done, or how to do it. And demonstrating how this shifts things for the better.

- Expressing a compelling vision yourself. And showing how you make sure that other people are able to contribute to the construction of that vision too.

I've often thought that JFK's 'We choose to go to the moon' speech is a great example of this. Kennedy sets out his vision for putting a man on the moon (and getting him home safely again) by the end of the decade. But instead of denying that there will be difficulties, he includes them. Saying, for example, that the ship will need to be 'made of new metal alloys, some of which have not yet been invented'.

Empire Builders will love this visionary approach. And they are often relieved to discover that, as a leader, they don't need to have all the answers or always be in control. Instead, it is their intention to help people find the way through together that needs to be strong. And that is something they can do very well.

Enforce a more collective approach

Build on the role modelling described earlier by making it non-negotiable that your Empire Builder takes a more collective approach to developing plans and agreeing on actions.

Having a more collective vision or plan is messy and in the short term it does risk the execution getting slowed down and diluted. In the long run though, that collective ownership and the wider, more substantial foundation it provides can make all the difference.

Your Empire Builder may feel threatened, or try to exclude you and is likely to deny that there's any need for it, so be ready for a response along the lines of: 'We haven't got time to consult everybody, we just need to get on with things.' But that is how tricky problems get ignored and opportunities get missed. Stand your ground and make sure that your Empire Builder is:

- Listening to colleagues at all levels in different parts of the organisation
- Including other sources of information that give a variety of viewpoints

- Not dismissing any dissenting voices and having a good process for dealing with (rather than excluding) any inconvenient problems or concerns they raise.

Mentor them on task management and systems thinking

An Empire Builder's primary *Attention focus* is on people and they are usually very good at understanding and delivering what people need in return for their loyalty and support. Because this is such a strength for them, they will often learn to rely on it more and more and fail to develop parallel skills around task management and systems thinking. Their over-reliance on other people to handle those factors makes their leadership vulnerable and one-dimensional and reinforces their tendency to overlook or wilfully ignore complicated issues.

If you have a difficult Empire Builder working for you, it's worth applying some time and resources to help them develop their skills in the following areas:

First, task management, including topics such as:

- Outcome focus (*what* and *how*, rather than exclusively *who*)
- Prioritisation – using tools like the Eisenhower Matrix
- Scheduling and project management – for deadlines and resource allocation
- Personal time management and organisation (so they don't get so distracted by attending to their followers).

Second, systems thinking. You'll want to encourage your Empire Builder to start thinking about how the different aspects of your organisation relate to and interact with each other, perhaps considering the following:

- Using a big-picture approach that considers relationships, connections and interactions.

- Using the McKinsey 7S framework[2] and other systems tools – it can be helpful to see that there's more to business and organisational success than getting people to follow you (although that is also an essential system in itself!).

Tips for colleagues and staff of Empire Builders

If you're working for or alongside an Empire Builder in the right circumstances then it can be an invigorating experience. Here is someone whose self-confidence and focus on what people need can bring lots of clarity, direction and motivation. Especially in times of uncertainty or when faced with a big opportunity.

When things aren't going so well, and their denial of problems or their tendency to overlook complications has led them to start taking control in the wrong way – to empire build – then it's a different experience entirely. At those times, when the Empire Builder has become difficult, then their *Excess* stress strategy will take some careful handling. Here are the tactics to consider if that's your situation.

How to disagree

An Empire Builder who has become difficult really doesn't like people telling them that something they've committed to won't work, or that it isn't the best thing to be doing. Or that it has some complications that will require them to seek help from people outside their control.

Here are three approaches that can help:

- **Build consensus first.** Do not be the only dissenting voice if you need to disagree with a difficult Empire Builder, or need to bring some troublesome news to their attention. Find allies with power in the organisation and test your views on them. Ask them for support and stay safe.

- **Copy their people focus.** Don't overwhelm an Empire Builder with details or with the complexity caused by an issue you've spotted. Instead, report on how things are impacting people. Or on how influential people might view things. This will get their attention at least.

- **Make good use of the 'Yes; And . . . ' tactic.** This helps to bounce difficult stuff straight back at your Empire Builder without directly disagreeing. You might say something like: *'Yes, of course, the plan of action you've committed us to could work. **And** there's this possibly tricky issue we might have to deal with first. [Say what it is.] How should we start tackling that?'*

Border patrol

For an Empire Builder who has become difficult at work, their empire building is often a means to an end. It brings things that they see as important into their control. It makes dissent harder. And it boosts their chances of winning acclaim. These are powerful motivations. In addition, organisations are sometimes complicit in that empire building, relying on someone charismatic to get more and more done.

But what if you're in a part of the empire that is about to get swept up into their control? Or what if *you* currently control that part of the business; what does that mean for you?

Make sure that you're patrolling the border regularly:

- What big projects or external issues might affect how your area is structured, and who reports to whom?

- Get as 'ahead of the game' as you can, so that you are connected to those with influence, understand where and how decisions are being made, and can make a compelling case about where your own contribution is best placed.

- If you need to put up a fight, who and what is on your side? Who are your allies? What arguments and other resources can you bring to bear? What do you control? When should you walk away?

Boundaries

Empire Builders are often very charismatic and sensitive to what makes people tick and are therefore great at getting people to go above and beyond in pursuit of their vision.

With this type of difficult person, a big part of operating healthy boundaries is about just being aware that you need to set and maintain boundaries at all. It's OK to get swept along, supporting a high-profile project or being part of a growing department. Just keep your eyes open as you go.

Here's what to look out for:

- Your specialist knowledge or your important credibility might get used to prop up something which hasn't been properly thought through or which can't work without awkward adjustments. And you might not be aware that this is happening.

- Are there power games being played in the background of what's happening around you? Different people vying for control in some way? It's possible to end up getting manipulated in that scenario, to be used as a pawn in someone else's game.

- Are you getting left with all the donkey work? Empire Builders aren't good at taking care of tricky tasks and details. Or at making sure things all join up. Instead, they will rely on their loyal colleagues and followers to do those things while they glamorously spearhead a project.

Don't be complicit in or get used by someone else's empire building without giving your explicit consent. And make sure that you are proactive in getting what you need as well. If that doesn't work, be prepared to revisit the first two tips above.

Growth tips for Empire Builders

If you're a leader-mentor, a coach or a human resources professional who wants to help an Empire Builder to grow, this section covers the directions you might want to take and offers some tips for the content you might cover.

Resistance to overcome

Empire Builders are charismatic (on the outside, anyway) and powerful people. They may resist attempts to help them grow and be very strongly charming about it. It can be useful to consider the following points.

- **Make sure you've done your own growth work.** Empire Builders are very sensitive to what's going on in others and will use their intuition to detect if you have a similar gap between how you're projecting and how you're feeling on the inside. If they spot that, you'll lose credibility.

- **The real growth opportunities for Empire Builders are internal, not external.** This isn't surprising, because we know that they're already good at doing the external part – that's how they grow their empires! They may therefore resist doing internal work until you direct them to consider the benefits. See more about this in the section on Mindset shifts below.

- **Do *not* collude** in their empire building and their self-propaganda. Instead, be a critical friend; on their side but not blinded by their charms.

Skills development: tasks and systems

I've covered this earlier in the Tips for leaders section, so check out the suggested content there. Your goal should be to unlock some learning for your Empire Builder around task management and systems thinking.

Empire Builders have often not tackled this kind of learning. Perhaps this comes from not having to, as their people skills are often so well developed, or perhaps it comes from unconscious attempts to mask feelings of self-doubt or shame (which I've covered below). In either case, I've found that even Empire Builders who are being experienced as difficult at work are usually open to the new possibilities that this learning can bring them.

Mindset shifts

Perhaps more than most of the other types of difficult people, Empire Builders can often have a pretty large gap between the confidence and charisma they project and how they actually feel on the inside. There are two related areas to address.

First, learning to co-exist with self-doubt

Self-doubt is the mechanism that most often derails an Empire Builder's attempts to develop more flexibility in their approach. In essence, that lack of flexibility is a side effect of their over-reliance on their people skills. Rather than feeling confident (on the inside) that they can manage tasks and systems as well as they manage people, they may have instead come to unconsciously believe that they *cannot* do so. It's crucial therefore that you help them to successfully co-exist with this self-doubt.

Help them to:

1 Be aware of their **internal dialogue**, which might be saying things like:

- *'I can't do good time management.'*
- *'I won't be able to project-manage that myself.'*
- *'I couldn't cope with keeping track of how everything is connected in our organisation.'*

2 Be more consciously aware of their **feelings** of self-doubt and/or the associated feelings of anxiety, worry and insecurity.

Self-doubt exists for a reason – it stops us from diving into a difficult task unprepared or from biting off more than we can chew. But it ceases to be useful when it puts unhelpful limits on what we believe ourselves to be capable of doing.

Once they have more self-awareness around this, it becomes much easier to see self-doubt for what it is. And to then choose whether or not it's more useful to be constrained by that self-doubt or to discover ways of dealing with it.

Second, dealing with the shame gap

Empire Builders are often unconsciously comparing themselves to some standard of magnificent, glorious leadership that in reality probably doesn't exist and is always going to be just out of reach. The gap between that kind of impossible external standard and what we really believe about ourselves, on the inside, can be an uncomfortable thing to live with.

At the right times, this gap can be a very strong and useful driver, making people strive to work faster, achieve more, be stronger or make fewer mistakes. At the wrong times, I believe it is the main cause of an Empire Builder's *Excess* stress response and a large part of what can make them seem difficult at work. Empire Builders may react to that gap by projecting more strength, seizing more control, crushing dissent and building up more and more of an empire.

More self-awareness and then conscious choice are the ways to deal with it.

Raise awareness by exploring whether your Empire Builder may be telling themselves something like this:

- *'If people only knew how weak and uncertain I feel, they wouldn't follow me.'*
- *'If they knew what I was really like, they certainly wouldn't like or respect me.'*

Once you have more of that awareness, explore the answers to these questions:

- Is the energy behind your motivation *mostly* coming from shame or from the fear of failure or looking bad?
- If so, could a different approach help you to be more effective overall?
- And, if you didn't have to be liked or respected, how might that make things easier for you at work?

The goal here is to raise awareness of what might be unconsciously driving them. And then to offer more choice about how they respond to those drivers.

Summary

- -

There's something very flattering and engaging about catching the attention of an Empire Builder at their best. You can almost hear yourself thinking how happy you'd be to follow their bold certainty and their interpersonal brilliance.

But it can go very wrong. When the issues are complex, if they put their own agenda above that of the organisation, or if helpful but dissenting voices are ignored, then things can get difficult at work. At those times, the Empire Builder can react badly, sweeping up control rather than building consensus and shooting the messenger rather than facing difficult and nuanced problems.

For leaders of Empire Builders who have become too difficult at work, there are three connected strands to changing the situation for the better. First, role modelling a more open version of inspirational leadership that includes rather than excludes doubts and concerns about uncertain, complex problems. Second, by enforcing a more collective and collegiate approach. Leaders mustn't be fooled into thinking that their only choice is to give an Empire Builder totally free rein. Last, use your own understanding of how organisations work to help round out their often underdeveloped skills in task- and systems management.

Colleagues and team members of difficult Empire Builders will need to know how to disagree with them in a way that is risk-free and effective. You'll need to build consensus, use a people-focused approach to presenting information and make good use of the 'Yes, And . . . ' tactic. You also need to make sure that you're not surprised, caught out or disadvantaged by their empire building. Colleagues and team members should keep their eyes open to boundary breaches too. Don't allow your knowledge or experience to be used to justify their actions. And don't get used as a pawn in someone's game or get left behind doing all the donkey work with nothing to show for it.

For those who want to help develop a difficult Empire Builder, personal credibility is important, since they're often so sensitive to what makes people tick. If you have credibility and can gain their trust, you can be a good critical friend. Use that to reinforce my earlier points about task- and systems-management skills. And when you have their trust, help them explore issues around self-doubt that might be keeping them stuck in that people-focused way of doing things. To get right into the heart of the matter, explore their shame gap, the sense of inadequacy that might really be driving their desire for empire.

The great strength of an Empire Builder is to use their charisma and the self-confidence they project to recruit people to their cause and then sweep through the difficult stuff like no one else can. When they can do this, be inspirational *and* include thorny, complex issues *and* include dissenting voices; then they can really become someone who makes the whole greater than the sum of its parts.

In the next chapter, we'll consider a very dissimilar type of difficult person at work. Someone whose confidence on the outside is altogether very different – the Worrier.

Notes

1 Turner, Ted (n.d.), as cited in 'Ted Turner quotes.' QuoteFancy. Last accessed 22 June 2023.

2 Waterman, R. H., Peters, T. J., & Phillips, J. R. (1982). In search of excellence: Lessons from America's best-run companies. New York, NY: Harper & Row.

chapter 16

Type 7 – The Worrier

'There is only one way to avoid
criticism: do nothing, say nothing,
and be nothing.'

Aristotle[1]

In a nutshell

The Worrier is usually a very conscientious and responsible person who takes their job seriously.

Key characteristics: They want to be helpful and to add value without needing to be in the limelight. They often have a good sense of right and wrong and are typically very detail-focused.

Why others can find them difficult: Issues at work can arise from a focus on what might go wrong and a struggle to see the bigger picture. These can lead to micromanaging, difficulties with influencing, and a sensitivity around protecting 'their' turf.

Example

Fiona manages a number of people and others are often impressed that she can remember so much detail about their work. She's quite serious and conscientious and likes to be helpful. She can be pretty tenacious in rooting out errors and making sure you don't do things by half. But it's not hard to see that underneath that she's often very concerned to not get things wrong; sometimes in a way that makes her overly nervous and controlling.

At their best

They will work tirelessly to make sure that their own output, and that of their teams, is as high-quality, watertight and comprehensive as possible. They seek out new opportunities to be helpful and can handle such a range and depth of detail that, through their teams, they can tackle a huge range of projects and issues simultaneously. They've learned to manage their own tendency to micromanage under stress and to see the bigger picture, moving things forward as well as making sure that no mistakes are made and that nothing is left to chance.

When do things get difficult?

Worriers bring to their work a strong focus on the task itself and tend to be highly conscientious and responsible people. When there is little stress or uncertainty in the wider environment, and when their leaders acknowledge them for what they bring and support them in how they might approach things, they can be powerfully productive.

When the situation is less clear or the way ahead demands some element of risk, and if they are under pressure, they can become hyper-focused on making sure no mistakes are made. At that point they may stop trusting their teams and colleagues to do things properly. As a result, they will often fall into an overbearing style of micromanaging. They are unlikely to have spent time building relationships for the sake of it and may have little interpersonal capital, thus finding it hard to work across departmental boundaries without being intrusive and controlling.

Leaders may begin to feel that their Worrier's anxious approach is counterproductive and makes them unreliable in the very situations when they need to be at their best.

Worriers are also likely to find it frustratingly hard to influence the agenda in board meetings and other decision-making bodies, as their communication style often relies on building up large quantities of detail.

Their place in the Matrix of Difficult People

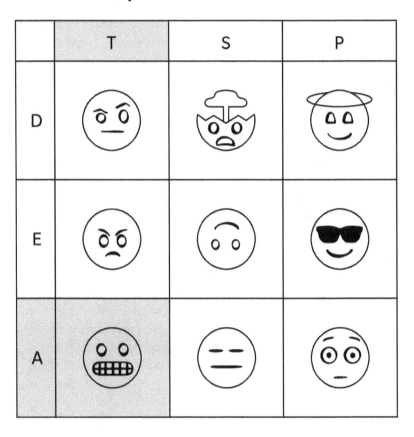

	T	S	P
D			
E			
A			

Attention Focus

Task – the Worrier's primary focus is on discrete tasks and they approach and assess their work and their team through that same lens.

Stress Strategy

Avoidance – under pressure, the Worrier will be doing their utmost to steer clear of making mistakes or of being criticised for the mistakes of others.

How to spot a Worrier

Micromanaging

Off all the types of Difficult People, the Worrier is the one most likely to develop a habit of micromanaging. It is the result of their natural preference for focusing on specific tasks, combined with a keen eye for detail and their typical stress response of seeking to avoid mistakes and criticism.

The micromanaging habit can be a little harder to spot if you're the boss of a Worrier. See how they interact with their team members and colleagues, including:

- What are their collaboration and delegation styles like (open and permissive or closed and prescriptive)?
- Is there an upwards and sideways flow of ideas and suggestions for improvement from their team and colleagues?

Lengthy and overly detailed presentations etc.

The Worrier's desire to avoid mistakes and criticisms includes those of omission as well as commission. If they're making a presentation, writing a report or briefing you on an issue, they will be acutely concerned that nothing is left out for which they could later be criticised. Because of this, they will often try to cover everything at once in everything they do. Look out for slides crammed with tiny font, reports filled with unnecessary appendices and verbal briefings that never seem to end.

'Hyper-focus' leading to unreliability

If you've ever watched or taught a child who is learning to ride a bicycle, you'll know that it can be very counterproductive to say 'Watch out for that pothole or that rock', as this often causes them to lock up and steer straight towards it! This is the phenomenon of hyper-focus; in this context, someone becomes so fixated on avoiding a problem or obstacle that they are unable to pay attention to anything else.

At work, the paradox of this phenomenon is that a Worrier who hasn't done the right kind of development can find themselves unable to steer around the obstacles and blind to the bigger picture and the relationships that are so important to success. For those reasons, bosses of Worriers who have become difficult at work may often experience them as unreliable; as an 'unsafe pair of hands' and may feel reluctant to trust them with anything challenging or out of the ordinary.

Tips for leaders of a Worrier

The unconscious pressures that a Worrier places themselves under can be much higher than their terrier-like attitude suggests and may hide a lot of anxiety and a desire for approval. Leaders who want to help a Worrier be at their best at work will need to look beyond the surface. If you can do that, and find ways to unstick a Worrier who has become difficult, then you'll have a very conscientious, focused and loyal member of your team.

Here's what to do.

Snowplough leadership

Snowplough leadership is the simple idea that, as a leader, your job is to shovel blockages out of people's way and make sure they've got enough grip on the road to make good progress.

Worriers can appear to be very tough and tenacious and if they're battering down doors to ferret out missing information, see if you have an easier way to open those doors, perhaps to colleagues and to different parts of the organisation.

Similarly, Worriers won't naturally realise that our grip on the organisational road is highly dependent on building and maintaining good relationships with a wide range of people. What opportunities can you create to introduce your Worrier to important people when there is no immediate task-focused requirement; just for the sake of establishing relationships?

Affirmation

I mentioned 'hyper-focus' earlier and our possible sense of a Worrier as seeming like an unsafe pair of hands because of it. For those reasons, it's really important for leaders to cover two areas within the broader concept of affirmation at work:

- First, do whatever you can to demonstrate to them that it's OK to sometimes metaphorically drop the ball in their work. Perhaps relate stories of your own experience and how you survived and learned from making mistakes.

- Second, your Worrier will need affirmation – which means expressing appreciation, encouragement and support for their ideas and contributions. You can also be strategic in how and what you affirm, using it to reinforce the behaviours you want to see more of, such as relationship building or self-management around anxiety.

Role modelling an empowering delegation style

A Worrier's preferred style of delegation, particularly if they are being experienced as difficult, is all about control. They want to avoid any surprises, make sure nothing is missed and preclude any mistakes. Combined with their hard focus on tasks, this is likely to lead to micromanaging and to a spiral of low morale and disem-powered people. Which can then paradoxically bring about more errors and mistakes overall.

Leaders should role model a better, more empowering approach which:

- Emphasises the desired Outcome (the 'What'), rather than the process or method to be used (the 'How')

- Is about offering open and supportive reflection and guidance, so that they're a trusted partner in the work, rather than being an ever-vigilant overseer.

This will give their delegatees more autonomy and scope to work to their strengths, as well as more confidence that they can seek help if and when they need it.

Less is more in successful communication

With a natural focus on the minutiae of each individual task, and a desire to not miss anything out, Worriers who have become difficult at work will often unknowingly be switching people off by piling on detail after detail in everything they do.

However, there's evidence to suggest that the majority of people at work prefer to receive and process information at a big-picture level, rather than at a specific, detailed level. Worriers tend to be the oppo-site. This is both a strength, in that they can remember and process a lot of useful detail at once, and a weakness, in that they may not communicate and influence well with the majority of people who don't share their traits.

As a minimum, make sure that your Worrier is doing the follow-ing in their communications:

- Including executive summaries
- Establishing clear priorities
- Making well-defined conclusions or recommendation; and
- Not switching people off with too much detail or length.

You may need to tutor them (I've included some more Growth tips for them at the end of this chapter), but it's so important for their success as a member of your team that you could also consider making it a non-negotiable part of their development.

Career management

The final area that a leader might want to consider in dealing with a difficult Worrier at work is how much they want to guide their career steps.

It can be tough for someone whose stress response is *Avoidance* and who doesn't naturally do big picture to take a proactive approach to managing their own career. This might be why they sometimes get overlooked, stuck and sidelined.

Leaders might want to tackle some of these issues as part of their pastoral care of a Worrier:

- Looking further ahead than the next task or project; where are they going, longer term?

- They'll find it easy to focus on the career mis-steps that they want to avoid. But what are the opportunities (or even the risks) they might want to shoot for, in service of a longer-term career goal?

- Help them to be aware of the big-picture patterns and trends in your industry or profession. How do those trends relate to their career aspirations?

Tips for staff and colleagues of a Worrier

Being a team member or a colleague of a worrier can actually be fairly relaxing if you're in a stable environment, you share a bit of their characteristics around conscientiousness and responsibility, and you're not too concerned about altering the status quo. They'll be helpful and will make sure you're looked after. And they'll champion your cause if there's a minor injustice somewhere.

On the other hand, if there's some stress or external threat in the wider system, your Worrier is likely to get difficult quite quickly, and in a seemingly intractable way. Team members may find themselves being tightly micromanaged, with few usable opportunities to grow and develop. Colleagues and anybody else who is trying to lead a significant change may find their efforts frustrated by a long list of unknown risks that must first be addressed.

Here's what to do.

Dodge rather than placate

It may not be practically possible to address each and every point of concern that a Worrier might raise. This can be especially challenging if you're trying to lead on a change project or some other piece of work that needs their approval or support. You might even find that every issue you investigate just gives them more to worry about. Or that it sabotages your ability to communicate clearly and succinctly about the project by piling on more and more detail that must be covered.

Don't spend too much time pandering to or trying to placate this.

Instead, you need to dodge over or around them. But you need to do so in as collegiate a way as possible, asking for their priorities and assessing their concerns for yourself. Then, if necessary, use all of your allies and supportive colleagues, bosses and connections to go around or over your Worrier and get your project moving.

This will be much easier for colleagues of Worriers to do than it will for their team members, but the principles stand. Use in conjunction with the tips below.

Temporarily delegate upwards

If you're working for a Worrier who has slipped into micromanaging, it can be an incredibly demoralising experience. It can seem impossible to satisfy their concerns and hard to predict just what they want to achieve or what issues they will focus on next. This is because they often don't know what outcome they want, just that they want to avoid unknown mistakes and unforeseen omissions along the way.

To create some headroom, as a temporary relief from the scrutiny and to give you space to work on things that need to be achieved, learn how to delegate upwards to them. You can often get a micro-managing Worrier to take over the work themselves by using language like this:

- *'I'm a bit worried I might have missed some issues here, but I can't think what.'*
- *'This is 90 per cent done but I have a nagging feeling there are some problems that might need to be avoided down the line.'*
- *'How many of the potential issues should we cover; is it possible to exclude every risk or list everything that should be eliminated?'*

This tactic probably shouldn't be overused as it is not in everybody's interests to perpetuate things. But as a temporary relief, see if it works for you.

Fake going nuclear

Worriers are usually conscientious, helpful people who want to make a contribution in the workplace. They are also usually quite fair in their approach. For them, it is all about avoiding mistakes in the tasks. They think they're helping and won't necessarily be aware that they may also be unfairly demoralising their team members and blocking or frustrating the efforts of colleagues.

Most of the time, others respond to them with reason: 'Thank you, yes, I agree there could be risks here that we need to avoid. I'll re-work it.'

So it can be quite a useful wake-up call for them to have the impact of their micromanaging negativity reflected back to them in an unreasonable way. Be mindful of your situation and don't be rude or aggressive, but do have a loud and unignorable reaction to their latest micromanaging, risk-avoiding blockage. For example:

- Throw your papers on the desk.
- Loudly tell them something like this: *'I can't work like this anymore. If you know everything, do it yourself!'*

- Storm out and do not come back until they come to you.
- Do *not* use words such as, 'I quit'.

You're not quitting, you're expressing dissatisfaction in a way that can't be ignored. For a person who so desperately wants to avoid mistakes, they should be left with no doubt that they've made a big one.

This tactic has worked for me personally and for coaching clients on several occasions and is best done in cold blood. Force yourself to do it and fake the over-reaction, so that you're really still in control.

Manage your own development

You might find that under a Worrier you're not getting opportunities to grow and develop, not being suitably stretched by your work and not being exposed to helpful influences and role models.

If so, you'll need to make the headroom for those opportunities yourself. Volunteer outside work if you need to broaden your experience. Look for courses you can take in your own time as Worriers may sabotage things, for example by calling you back from training as soon as they start to feel exposed without you.

Growth tips for Worriers

Coaches, leader-mentors and human resources professionals who want to help a Worrier to grow can use this section to help shape their approach. Above all though, it's important to first create a safe space for a Worrier who has become difficult at work.

They'll be doubling down on their preferences to avoid mistakes and focusing hard on the tasks they're responsible for, so present this growth as an exploration, something where the journey and the learning along the way are as important as the destination.

Self-management

People who are naturally conscientious and responsible can often get pushed into the *Avoidance* stress strategy at work, either from being too far or too long outside their comfort zones, or from high levels of uncertainty in their wider environment.

It's essential then that Worriers build their self-management skills. In emotional intelligence terms, this is the ability to regulate emotions and behaviours in the service of goals. It includes being aware of emotions, managing stress and fostering a sense of well-being.

Simple practices which can make a significant difference for Worriers often include:

- **Journaling** – to build the skill of awareness as they are often tempted to bury their anxieties in busy work, leading to a vicious circle of more worries.

- **Time in nature** – studies show this helps one to be more resilient and to hold a healthy, wider perspective.

- **Balance** – they also need to prioritise interests which nurture their creative or caring sides, balancing the stresses and focus of work.

People focus

Worriers who have become difficult at work are typically overlooking the need to give enough of their *attention focus* to **People**. This can often create problems with their relationships and leaves them without a support structure. Here are the most important People focus areas for Worriers to develop:

- **Delegating better.** Worriers will often benefit from some training in a more empowering style of delegation. One which emphasises a focus on the desired outcomes, rather than the exact approach to be taken. This really helps to avoid micromanaging and also gives team members much more scope to play to their strengths.

- **Building relationships.** Worriers can tend to be a bit functional in their approach to relationships. Instead of building a network of loose connections, they might only prioritise the relationships they need for the immediate demands of the job. Worriers should take time to get to know a much wider range of people, at all levels in the organisation and outside it.

Practice being strategic

The conscientiousness, task focus and all-round helpfully serious nature of most Worriers can sometimes lead to a kind of heads-down, getting-on-with-the-job approach that doesn't do justice to their capabilities. Most would benefit from just raising their heads a little more often and getting a view of the bigger picture.

In practical terms, it can often be useful to:

- Reflect on the organisation's wider operating environment and see what's happening out there. A quality newspaper or trade journal is often the easiest way to do this. What are the big trends or disruptions?

- What key issues are currently affecting your whole organisation – and who is at the centre of those? Look at internal communications, official publications and internal briefings to help discover these.

Influencing and communications style

A Worrier's desire to be helpful and to add value can sometimes be cancelled out by their communication and influencing styles. This might include presentations crammed with tiny fonts, facts and figures; reports with weighty appendices 'just in case'; extended verbal briefings.

A Worrier who recognises any of those traits could use the points below to experiment with a more effective and influential communication style:

- Always start with the big picture of your message, since the majority of people at work prefer to start there too. Only drill down further if people need you to. They may already be in agreement.

- For the same reason, summarise your key points at the beginning.

- Always draw clear conclusions – no sitting on the fence and hoping that others will reach the conclusions from the mass of data you have provided.

- Make sure that priorities and recommendations are clearly identified. If you present *everything* as a priority, then people will tend to assume *nothing* is.

- Include diagrams and illustrations, as a majority of people at work like to visually 'see' a product, service or idea in order to be convinced by it.

Summary

- -

The terrier-like nature of a Worrier, digging and biting and tugging at something until all of the mistakes are revealed and all of the risks are mitigated, hides quite a high level of anxiety.

In the wrong circumstances, their tendency to try and avoid getting anything wrong or missing anything out can lead to disempowering micromanagement and poor communication. As well as a sense that they are unreliable, since their hyper-focus on not making a mistake can cause them to fluff their lines or to drop the ball at critical moments.

For leaders of a Worrier it's important to look beyond their surface attitude and address their need for affirmation. They'll also need help connecting to parts of the organisation where they haven't established good relationships. They'll need to see that you are supportive, that your own leadership creates a safe space where they can ease off from being ever vigilant. You'll probably also want to mentor them in developing a more empowering delegation style and a more effective communication style. Last, you might want to encourage them to raise their heads and consider their longer-term career trajectory, as they're unlikely to do this without prompting.

For colleagues and team members of a Worrier, if there's some stress in the system you might find them to be quite intractable and difficult. It can be hard to satisfy each point of concern they raise and you may need to learn how to dodge rather than placate this trait in order to make progress on a project. Create some headroom by delegating back up to them if you need the temporary relief of some space to work in your own style. Used sparingly and in a controlled manner, the 'go nuclear' approach can give them a useful wake-up call and rapidly shift their behaviour towards you for the better. Make sure you also manage your own career development.

For those who want to help develop a Worrier most of the above points also apply. Create a safe space and encourage self-management practices so that they're not always forced into the **Avoidance** stress strategy. Give them some guidance on developing their people focus, especially in delegating and in building relationships. And help them to think more strategically, both in having a big-picture view of the organisation as a system and in presenting data in a more concise and influential way.

The true strengths of a Worrier are not really that far from the surface. They are great at making sure nothing is missed and at applying their conscientiousness to produce high-quality, comprehensive work. As a leader, they're responsible, fair and supportive. As a team member and colleague, they're naturally helpful and are unconcerned with hogging the limelight. All of those strengths can be set free when they learn to manage their concerns and to manage their relationships with others more consciously and effectively. And that shift from terrier-like guard dog to team-leading Labrador is definitely worth supporting.

In the next chapter we'll meet a Difficult Person at work who can be a little harder to shift, unless they want to – the Rock.

Note

1 Aristotle (n.d.), as cited in 'Top 100 Inspirational Quotes', Ed. Kevin Kruse, Forbes, 2013. Last accessed 22 June 2023.

chapter 17

Type 8 – The Rock

'A diamond is just a chunk of coal that
did well under pressure.'

Henry Kissinger[1]

In a nutshell

The Rock is usually a highly responsible and committed person, with a deep sense of loyalty to the organisation.

Key characteristics: They'll be quietly and steadily doing whatever it takes to ensure that important systems and processes are running properly.

Why others can find them difficult: Issues at work can arise because of their silent and immovable refusal to do anything that might expose the business to risk, especially if they believe that someone hasn't understood the knock-on consequences of a course of action.

Example

Peter takes his job seriously and prefers it when he and his team are left to get on with things. He works hard to make sure that nothing goes wrong in the business and is often the one that others rely on to patch a problem. People get frustrated with him when, instead of responding positively to their requests for change, he complains about all the other things that must happen first, with which he says his team are already overloaded.

At their best

Rocks are the true stalwarts of any business. Self-motivated, responsible and with a healthy balance, so that the job of keeping everything going is rewarding and sustainable for them and their teams. They've learned to apply their understanding of interconnected systems beyond their own immediate area, to include the wider organisation. And by combining that understanding with effective influencing, they also help other senior leaders to look ahead and avoid problems, providing a solid foundation for success at work.

When do things get difficult?

The Rock wants systems and processes at work to be on a sound footing and will probably be doing a lot of behind-the-scenes improvised maintenance to make sure they keep ticking over nicely. When they are appreciated for this, and their concerns about any shortcomings are taken seriously, they are stalwarts of the workplace.

Things are likely to get difficult, however, when the systems and processes at work are not quite up to best practice and there are either changes under consideration or there's a refusal to acknowledge a critical problem. Then they may become less stalwart and more stubbornly rock-like.

Their concern is that nobody else really seems to understand how everything fits together and which bit of a system or process depends on something else. So that, in order to change one thing – introduce a new business practice for example – there are a half-dozen other supporting things that must be addressed first. Their motivation is to *avoid* damage and risks to the organisation and they will often be low-key advocates for fixing things.

If you ask, for example, *'How's it going with implementing the new database?'* they may answer quite honestly, *'It's going well. Quite a lot of work, but we're really putting in the hours.'* But you may not realise that they are actually tidying up the **old** database, or putting right errors that mustn't be carried over before they will even consider the new one.

Unfortunately, the end result can often seem to be a block to progress or a cause of long behind-the-scenes delays.

Their place in the Matrix of Difficult People

	T	S	P
D			
E			
A			

Attention Focus

Systems focused – the Rock's primary focus, and the way in which they approach and assess things, is on interconnected systems and how these mesh together. This is partly why they can often see problems in what (to others) are apparently straightforward solutions.

Stress Strategy

Avoidance – under pressure, the Rock will seek to avoid risks to the business, using their knowledge of the systems and processes at work to uncover problems that need addressing.

How to spot a Rock

Caught between a hard place and a rock

Some people report this sense of being trapped between two sources of pressure.

On the one side a board or management team of colleagues who are expecting them to deliver a step-change in the business. On the other side, a team led by a Rock that seems impossible to convince of the required course and speed of action.

People say that their interactions with the Rock leave them feeling as if they have failed to understand the significance of anything and are dangerously trying to pile on the straw that will break the camel's back. Or that their efforts to direct the Rock's team around any problems are met with passive resistance and they'll just add your instructions to their list of things that they know need doing and carry on as they were.

Complaining

Rocks are systems-focused people. They understand how the different elements of an organisation interact with and influence each other. But they can also forget that not everybody gets this. And perhaps because of that forgetfulness, and the pressure of keeping everything ticking over, they often seem to be bad at communicating upwards effectively. The end result is that key stakeholders can ignore things that are only functioning because of huge behind-the-scenes efforts.

What you might notice instead of good communication is a stream of what can seem like complaints: about just what is required; about how much pressure their team is under; and about the riskiness of your proposals.

Delays to your delays

The need that a Rock perceives very strongly, to fix or maintain what is currently at risk before doing something else, is likely to extend the original (and perhaps uninformed) timeframes of your project. And to extend them again as more issues are discovered.

You rely on them to plug away

Rocks are people who are a good foundation. They're responsible and loyal and they want to quietly make sure things work properly so that problems and risks to the business are avoided. This naturally leads them to put in some long hours and to expect the same of their teams. In the normal course of things, they may not mention any of this but may just keep on doing it, behind the scenes.

Tips for leaders of a Rock

Most of the time leading a Rock will be easy – solid even. They'll probably have deep expertise in their sphere, won't need much external motivation, and can be trusted to get on with it. It's a joy to work with someone in that sweet spot.

Things can get difficult in the presence of the three factors I described earlier:

- Systems and processes that are perhaps not quite up to scratch
- Lots of work for the Rock and team to do just to keep things running; and
- A desired change accompanied by a lack of open consideration about everything that might be required to successfully implement it.

In those situations your Rock can become difficult to lead. Here's what to do about it.

Don't be superficial

Some of the Rocks that I've coached with had a belief that their leaders would come and go around them. Almost like the waves and the tide washing over an actual rock in the sea. This is a demanding challenge for leaders to overcome. Actions speak louder than words here and leaders can demonstrate that by:

- **Showing commitment** – show that you're willing to dig in and do what it takes to understand the issues they're concerned about.
- **Taking responsibility** – find something you can do, *hands on*, to help deal with some of those issues yourself.

Bridge the gap

If you have a Rock working for you who isn't great at communicating upwards, you might need to proactively bridge the gap.

The issue seems to be one that affects people who intuitively 'get' how the different elements of a system or an organisation mesh together and who are also busy keeping all that going. It seems they often lack the time and perhaps also the interpersonal touches that are needed to explain and convince others about the complexity and extent of any improvement or change projects.

Because of this, leaders who are feeling frustrated by both a lack of progress and a sense of not really knowing why this is happening might want to act as champions to their Rock with their own colleagues and bosses. Champion your Rock by:

- Using your own communication skills to help make the case around the salient points to your colleagues

- Smoothing out the relationship paths between your Rock and your own colleagues and bosses, and encouraging those people to get more involved in the issues too.

Include the wider strategic-management processes

I've made progress working with Rocks who have become difficult by helping them to expand the horizon of their systems thinking. This is important as what they're often doing is unconsciously lowering their gaze. They want to avoid risks or stop anything going wrong for the organisation, so they focus down onto those elements of its systems and processes over which they have direct control.

But that approach doesn't always reveal the whole picture of organisational life. For example: decisions that have to be made with imperfect information; or opportunities that have to be grasped quickly, even if they will stretch capabilities. In other words, that some risks do have to be taken.

It's sometimes too easy for a Rock to blame others for compromising when it's perhaps just a part of how organisations need to function. Leaders can help by:

- Opening up access to how you and your senior colleagues make decisions

- Checking that you're not placing impossible demands on them. Is it actually possible for them to do what's been asked of them? And how do you know?

- Checking that you're not giving contradictory messages about what's needed. Are you perhaps saying things like, 'I know this is daft, but the board have told us we have to do it.'? If so, it would be better positioned as 'We're making conscious compromises that we know involve some risk. And I need your support to make the most of it.'

Pastoral care

Pastoral care can be a tricky one for leaders of Rocks. They're so responsible that you can't really relieve them of anything. Saying 'You look tired. Go home and deal with this tomorrow' probably won't work with a Rock and may just add more stress. Yet they are likely to be quietly putting in long hours, worrying about how some key system or process might break overnight – and expecting their teams to do the same.

It becomes more a question of balance, I believe. In addition to offering the kind of support described earlier in this section, leaders can help by:

- Having open conversations about their balance and the sustainability of their and their team's efforts
- Offering recognition so that they know (even if they prefer to work in the background) that what they are doing is appreciated.

Tips for colleagues and staff of Rocks

In a well-run department or organisation in a steady-state situation, you'll love working with a Rock. As a colleague they'll be a safe, responsible and loyal ally: quietly advocating for fixes; making sure they support the smooth functioning of the processes and systems you all rely on. As your boss in those situations, you'll find them keen to provide a really solid foundation for you to work at your best, stay balanced, and manage your professional development.

At other times working for or alongside a Rock can get difficult. That's often when things aren't so well run or existing systems and management processes aren't as good as they need to be, and especially if there are change initiatives underway that the Rock feels have been inadequately considered. At those times, your experience of a Rock is likely to be characterised by intransigence, inflexibility and an intense feeling of being pressed for time.

Here are some tactics to help improve things.

The avoidance persuasion style

How do you successfully collaborate with a Rock who has become difficult at work? It's particularly tricky if they're being inflexible and won't react to external authorities, such as board directives or to requests from another senior leader.

The answer is to appeal to their desire to avoid issues which might expose the business to risk or which could damage how it functions. This means positioning things as being necessary to avoid or solve a problem.

For example, instead of:

- *'Can your team help out with Project X? It's going to transform the way we do things.'*

You could say:

- *'We need some help making sure this part of Project X doesn't go wrong please.'*

Or, instead of:

- *'The Finance Director has said you need to help us work out the costings for Project A.'*

You could ask:

- *'Can I have some support with Project A so that the costings don't cause any problems down the line?'*

Your credibility

A Rock will be unconsciously assessing whether or not you're a responsible, committed, problem-avoiding person like them. The key to getting on well with a Rock is to bring to the surface the parts of yourself which genuinely reflect those traits. And to emphasise them in what you do and how you talk with the Rock. Almost everybody will have their own aspect or flavour of them, so you don't need to be fake about it, just add some helpful approaches into your repertoire.

For example, you might want to demonstrate:

- **Responsibility** – by making sure you always do what you've said you would do.

- **Long-term commitment** – by ensuring that you're also considering what happens *after* the thing you're currently working on is done.

- **Systems thinking** – by seeking to understand the wider implications of what you're working on. Organisations are a bit like the plumbing in a big, old house. If you add an extra radiator in one room, the temperature and pressure might drop somewhere else. A Rock is usually very good at seeing that kind of interconnectedness.

- **Problem-avoidance** – by looking at what might go wrong as well as what needs to be achieved.

Boundaries

Rocks tend to move very much at their own pace – usually slow but unstoppable. As well as for their leaders, this raises boundary issues for their colleagues and for their team members.

For colleagues, you may need to be more proactive than usual in keeping an eye on how things are progressing. For example, if you're working on a joint project or are dependent on the Rock and their team to produce something for you, make sure that you're:

- **Actively involved in its project management**, including knowing the key milestones and deadlines, being prepared to call in support earlier rather than later; and

- **Be alert to delays**. Don't just assume progress will happen as you've agreed, as they may uncover risks and issues that they then prioritise over and above your needs.

As a team member of a Rock, you will need to make sure that their grind-it-out approach doesn't mean that you are getting leaned on to work long hours:

- Be clear about how much time you're prepared to put in and stick to a reasonable working timetable.
- Make sure you protect your time away from work.

Rocks are usually quite protective of their team members, so you probably won't experience opposition to this once you make them aware of it. It's just that they may otherwise assume they can always lean on you.

Out of the shadow of a Rock

Sometimes the perception of a Rock who has become difficult is that of someone who is unhelpful and intransigent. It's important for team members to make sure they don't inherit that perception too. Take opportunities to meet or speak directly with colleagues outside your immediate department. And if your boss causes a conflict, avoid taking sides and make them responsible for resolving it.

Growth tips for Rocks

If you're a coach, leader-mentor or human resources professional who wants to help, here are some of the main topics to cover in supporting a Rock to grow.

Resistance

In a fairly rock-like fashion, you may experience some resistance to growth work of this kind. Don't collude by agreeing with them. And don't argue with them either – it's very hard to move a Rock that doesn't want to be moved. This kind of resistance is about fear. Fear of the consequences (good and bad) if they do change – or if they try and it goes wrong.

Here's the kind of resistance you might notice:

Self-sabotage – comments along the lines of

- *'I don't have the time.'*
- *'That's just the way things are around here.'*

Exaggerating:

- *'I've tried before and it never works.'*
- *'Something always gets in the way.'*

Help them to overcome their fears by acknowledging that these are genuine concerns. And then focus on the risks of their *not* growing. What might go wrong then? What are the risks if everything continues as it is for them?

Raising and widening horizons

Rocks are sometimes baffled by or extremely dismissive of the higher-level risks, uncertainties and resource constraints that go into senior management decisions.

But it's not reasonable for Rocks to expect others to understand the difficulties and efforts involved in making sure *their* key systems and processes don't go wrong – if they won't put some effort into mastering those parts of the wider system which use, direct and fund them.

It's sometimes useful therefore to encourage a Rock to discover more of how their organisation functions at those levels across and up from their own. For example, by:

- Talking to colleagues informally about their priorities, concerns and ambitions

- Asking to attend board meetings and management committees to understand more of what needs to be juggled at that level.

Communication skills to develop

In addition to the discovery involved in raising and widening their horizons, you could also support a Rock in developing their ability to communicate their own concerns upwards more effectively.

There are two related areas which are perhaps worth exploring with them first:

- Building relationships

  It's much easier to communicate a complex and difficult problem if people already know and trust them. Do they personally know the appropriate influential people in the organisation – and vice versa? What opportunities do they have to make an impression – and what kind of impression do they want to make?

- Communication styles

  The most helpful aspects for a Rock are about using anything which boils complex issues down into the really important points. Senior leaders are almost always time-poor, so the Rock needs to make sure they rank priorities and use diagrams, summaries, tables and infographics to convey complex information clearly.

Maintaining a healthy balance

Rocks at work seem to internalise the pressures a lot. On the outside, they're dependable. The one who holds everything together while the storm breaks around them. On the inside, the strain of grinding away and the frustrations at not being able to persuade people about what's needed to make a change can take their toll.

If they haven't already discovered their own version of healthy balance, the downsides are burnout, health problems, decreasing effectiveness, poor relationships and ultimately failure.

As part of their development, it is worth checking how well balanced a Rock is feeling by having a fairly open conversation about their approach to balance:

- What a healthy balance looks like for them
- What strategies they have for staying resilient – exercise, hobbies, time off
- What kind of support networks are available to them – family, friends, etc.

Rock and roll careers

Under stress, Rocks are risk-avoiders and perhaps this is why they are not always as proactive at managing and directing their careers as they might be. But it is important that they don't let their careers be determined solely by others or allow the landscape to shift around them without responding.

If you can include some careers discussion, it might be very useful to a Rock who wants to grow at work to experiment with the following:

- Attend trade shows, read relevant publications, and seek out other ways to get to know what their kind of work is like in general, beyond the boundaries of their current organisation.
- Reach out and connect with people in their industry or in similar roles in other industries. Learn about their specific experiences at work and how they've approached their careers.

These are just simple and sensible first steps that anyone might take to be more proactive with their careers without any risk to the status quo.

Summary

A responsible loyal person who understands the fragility of what holds things together doesn't just give up under pressure. Instead, they dig in like a Rock and start steadfastly working through the things they can control, trying to weather the storm without letting everything get washed away.

As that happens, they can make their leaders feel superficial for wanting to go further or faster. At those times, leaders need to demonstrate their own commitment, so that they can begin to shift their Rock. Leaders may also want to bridge the gap back to the mainland, helping colleagues and other parts of the organisation to appreciate the scale and complexity of any change initiatives. And because the Rock finds it hard to look up under pressure, leaders may need to involve them in the wider strategic-management process, so that they understand the conflicting priorities that senior leaders have to juggle. Finally, Rocks can sometimes sacrifice their self-care and leaders should point them towards a more healthily balanced approach.

Colleagues and team members of a Rock may find them frustratingly inflexible and unwilling to respond to anything other than their existing priorities. Successful collaboration with a Rock requires two things. First, to make sure that every need is communicated in terms of the problems it will fix or the risks it will avoid. Second, to build genuine credibility by emphasising those aspects of yourself that are responsible and loyal, and to make sure you understand the interconnected dependencies of your projects. Watch out that their careful 'grind away' approach doesn't delay or derail a project. Or that it doesn't place unsustainable demands on your own time and effort. And, for team members especially, make sure that you're not in the shadow of your Rock and are not being seen as intransigent by those who matter.

Anybody who wants to help a Rock to grow and develop will probably need to overcome some resistance due to a fear of the consequences of change. Then help the Rock to raise their horizons so they can shift from complaining about to understanding the bigger picture of their organisation. Tutor them in effective communication, so they can help others to grasp the complexities and demands of their work. And support them in discovering a healthy balance, rather than internalising and ignoring the pressures they might be under. Last, encourage them to look up and outwards occasionally, not letting their own career be something that just washes over them.

With the right approach, a Rock can bring their real strengths to bear. They'll be looking ahead, alert to potential problems, and will be effective champions for dealing with them or for implementing best practices. They'll be a supportive leader and colleague, balancing the needs of the work with the needs of themselves and their people. And they'll help to connect the organisation's strategic priorities with the step-by-step implementation of what needs to be done. In that way, a Rock stands as a great foundation for long-lasting organisations and for impactful careers.

In the next chapter is a person who can become difficult at work not because they sometimes refuse to shift, but because they hesitate to shift others – the People Pleaser.

Note

1 Kissinger, Henry (n.d.), as cited in 'Pressure', Xaviroca, November 2021. Last accessed 22 June 2023.

chapter 18

Type 9 – The People Pleaser

**'The standard you walk past becomes
the standard you accept.'**

David Morrison[1]

In a nutshell

The People Pleaser is usually a warm self-effacing person who has built up a real depth of experience and a wide network of trusted and trusting connections.

Key characteristics: They value harmony and teamwork, and want their area to do well. They like to keep people onboard so they can make incremental improvements.

Why others can find them difficult: Issues at work can arise when they are avoiding conflicts, overlooking big changes that might rock the boat, or not actively contributing to the wider agenda, so that risks are undeclared and opportunities missed.

Example

Sam has worked in the industry for some time and she's the one to go to if you need a contact or a lead somewhere, because so many people know her and trust her. She believes that people are happiest at work if they're not having to deal with constant changes. Sam prefers to avoid confrontation or making waves and she's sometimes been taken advantage of or has failed to deliver something important because of this.

At their best

If People Pleasers have had the leadership support and done the development work suggested in this chapter, they are exemplary team leaders and great ambassadors for their organisation. The standards they set mean that people will happily rally around them. They'll build on that by continuously improving performance as well as driving step-changes when possible. And they'll use their relationship skills and their extensive trusted network to make valuable contributions right across the business.

When do things get difficult?

The People Pleaser has a gift for keeping everything steady and harmonious. When there are no thorny problems around, they'll use their team- and harmony-building abilities to steadily improve performance at work. This is a real strength and should not be discounted, even in the face of the potential problems described below.

Things can get difficult, however, when issues arise that might require a different approach to that steady harmony. If those issues require them to confront people, be highly directive with them or otherwise create conflict, then they may avoid doing so for quite some time, even if that creates risks and problems elsewhere in the business. Similarly, they may also avoid even positive changes which might disrupt that sense of steadiness. On rare occasions in order to avoid tackling those issues, they may instead take expedient short-cuts, dodging (or at least delaying) the issue.

They like to not make waves, wanting instead to have a bubble of smooth sailing in which they and their team can practise and steadily improve. But this also means that a People Pleaser may ignore opportunities that might be beneficial to the business as a whole, if not to their own area. Or that they may not report risks upwards in case somebody gets upset. They may also acquiesce too easily, saying yes to any direction their boss suggests, for a harmonious life. The impact of this approach is that the business can miss out on their expertise and connections just when it might need them.

Their place in the Matrix of Difficult People

	T	S	P
D	🙂	😱	😇
E	😠	🙃	😎
A	😬	😑	😳

Attention Focus

People focused – the People Pleaser's primary focus at work is on people and in particular, how well the people in their immediate surroundings appear (on the surface at least) to be getting on with each other.

Stress Strategy

Avoidance – under pressure, the People Pleaser will try to avoid anything which might create conflict or disrupt the smooth and harmonious environment they prefer.

How to spot a People Pleaser

Dodging the tough calls

People Pleasers are often reluctant to take a tough and uncompromising line on anything. If you've asked them to do something which requires that, they're unlikely to disagree with you. But they may say things like, 'Leave it with me, I'll find a way to sort it out.' And then avoid doing it, or try to do it in a way that doesn't upset the applecart.

Signs of *dis*-harmony in their team

You can't create teams that perform well together over the long run without setting and then holding people to clear behavioural standards. This creates a paradox for a People Pleaser who thrives on having a harmonious team around them and yet finds it hard to enforce those standards. Complaints or other signs of dissatisfaction among a small minority of their team members may indicate that some people are suffering from the permitted bad behaviour of one or two others.

An apparent lack of confidence in pushing the envelope

Some leaders have reported a frustrating sense that their People Pleaser could be so much more. That they have specialist knowledge or valuable connections that could benefit the whole business but which aren't really being used. Those leaders say it feels like their People Pleaser lacks the confidence to make the most of their resources and to push things faster and further.

Tips for leaders of a People Pleaser

Leading a People Pleaser who isn't under stress and who isn't avoiding any tough decisions or disruptive actions will be a pleasure. You'll see how easily people rally around them. Your business will benefit from the trust that suppliers and customers old and new are willing to place in them. And there'll be no ego on display for you to tiptoe around.

But when that isn't the case and they've become difficult to work with, here are some actions that leaders might want to take.

Test out their agreement with you

It's habitual for a People Pleaser to agree with their boss. At least, to your face. But that apparent acquiescence might be masking either a disagreement with your approach or their inability to actually do it. On some occasions, it might also be hiding an unconscious intention to take an expedient shortcut instead.

With a People Pleaser, leaders need to be sure they are not being 'pleased'. They have to tread the fine line between not taking agreement at face value and not displaying *dis*-trust or knocking confidence. The trick is to use open questions.

First, test out any concerns they may have about avoiding disharmony. For example, you could ask:

- *'What will be the impact of this on people? And will it be negative for any of them?'*
- *'What kind of disruptions might this cause to the way things are currently running?'*

Second, reduce the scope for them to avoid the tough parts, by holding them accountable:

- *'What's the first step you want to take towards this?'*
- *'And when will that happen, and how will I know?'*

Give support for the tough interpersonal issues

Leaders can also really help a People Pleaser by being a little more proactive than usual in the support they offer. It's perhaps a role-modelling opportunity as well, a chance to show them that you expect:

- That tough interpersonal calls have to be made
- That they can be done in a way that is sensitive and supportive.

There are lots of examples where a People Pleaser might need support on a difficult interpersonal issue. A critical supplier who isn't quite delivering what is needed but who is nonetheless important. A valued customer who wants unworkable changes to a significant project objective, mid-project. A senior member of staff with crucial skills who is being difficult at work. To offer support in those situations, here's what to do.

Dive down into their approach with them:

- How are they planning to approach this tricky interpersonal issue?

- What might their concerns about doing it be (you're trying to get to the bit they might avoid here)?
- Share how you've approached this kind of issue in the past – what worked, what was difficult, what do you wish you'd avoided?

Make it acceptable for disharmony and disruption to result in the short term; for example, by:

- Telling them how you will support them if and when that happens
- Brokering access to other support (for example, make sure they have the backing of a human resources professional in dealing with a difficult member of staff)
- De-briefing any learning from the experience, as part of your leadership coaching of their professional development.

Get them involved

Being likeable at work is often an underrated ability. For example it's especially useful in business development, recruitment and heading up in-house support functions. Leaders would do well to make sure they're adding at least a little bit of people-pleasing to their strategy and implementation. This can be particularly useful if a leader's own *Attention focus* is on tasks or systems and not people.

However, because they are both self-effacing and prefer to avoid making waves, a People Pleaser may not come forward with ideas or add their weight to the wider strategic agenda without a bit of prodding. In my experience, they are keen to help if asked and the barriers to them doing so are more that their views might be quieter, less pushy and less contrary than others. Because of that, leaders will need to listen carefully to what they have to say in order to get the most from it.

Two broad areas where their contributions might be helpful are:

- Exploring ways in which a more organic, less disruptive approach might contribute to setting and achieving your organisation's goals

- Considering the Strengths, Weaknesses, Opportunities and Threats (SWOT) of your business's people relationships. Both internally, in your people strategy, and externally, in the way that you build and manage key relationships.

Championing and encouraging to influence

A team led by a People Pleaser can sometimes be taken for granted. As long as everybody else is getting what they need – that is, is being pleased – that team and the People Pleaser themselves may be overlooked. This means they may not have the influence they need to acquire resources, access development opportunities, or add to decisions which affect them.

All of the types of difficult people on the Avoidance row of my matrix need coaching in how to influence upwards to some extent. But for a People Pleaser, this need is perhaps more likely to go un-noticed, against a background of apparent harmony.

Leaders can help by making sure that they both champion the People Pleaser and their team to the rest of the organisation and that they take opportunities to coach them on the importance of influ-encing the wider agenda. They'll be good at this because of their relationship skills. But they might just need a prod to do it.

Tips for colleagues and staff of People Pleasers

When it's good, the experience of working alongside a People Pleaser will be mostly okay. It can be useful and you can learn and benefit from it, if you're proactive. On the downside, their tendency to tol-erate poor behaviour for the sake of harmony and to avoid making waves in the wider agenda can cause some really big issues. Here are some tactics that can help in either situation.

Be alert to poor performance from their team

If you're a colleague of a People Pleaser you might find things very frustrating when you have a joint project or workstream that relies on them or their team. That's because, at heart, a People Pleaser is an incrementalist. They may delay, dodge or otherwise avoid dealing with anything that involves a significant change of pace, direction or approach.

To counter this issue, take the following steps:

- Break down the activities you're asking them to contribute to into smaller chunks so that you'll know sooner rather than later if a delay is occurring.

- Agree with them on some simple measures for those activities – how will you know when it's finished? How will you know if it's been done properly?

- Don't put up with unsatisfactory work or behaviours from a member of their team.

- Show your *dis*-pleasure if something isn't right or isn't working.

Proactively leverage their network

A People Pleaser's desire to avoid any confrontations or disruptions to the steady harmony of their department and team can mean that they're not a particularly proactive ally. This is a shame because they've often built up a deep understanding of their field, based on a wide network of trusted connections.

In fact, they should be your go-to person for anything which is about leveraging a network.

They will be happy to help you, but you will need to ask. You may also need to prove that you can be sensitive about the relationships they've established.

Examples of the help you might ask for would include:

- New business opportunities that might come from referrals in their network

- Discovering industry insights, trend-spotting and events to attend, using their connections' knowledge
- Recruitment, especially from hard-to-reach groups or just without advertising
- Collaborations with potential partners for any kind of mutual-interest project.

Boundaries

If you're part of a People Pleaser's team, problems can arise when other members of the team are not being held to account for how they're behaving. This could be as simple as times when they're not really pulling their weight. Or it could be more serious, when their behaviour might repeatedly be going beyond what is acceptable in the workplace.

Do not put up with or suffer in silence from any of this.

If it's a relatively minor issue and does not breach accepted standards, ask your manager to address it, making sure that you:

- Do this sooner rather than later.
- Stress that you're not experiencing a fair and friendly environment.
- Explain that you don't feel able to trust the problem person and can't rely on them to be part of the team.

However, if they brush you off, ask you to 'Not make a fuss', or repeatedly promise and then fail to tackle it – and always if the issue is a serious one – you'll need to take it further. No one has to work in an environment which is unsafe or disrespectful to them. If that's your situation seek guidance and as a minimum:

- Enlist the support of human resources professionals in your organisation.
- Keep notes about what is happening.
- Share your concerns with a trusted ally and/or another senior leader.
- Seek advice from your union or other representative or professional body.

The pluses and minuses of your own development

Chances are, it'll be a good overall experience working for a People Pleaser. However, in terms of your own career and development, there are some pluses and some minuses.

On the plus side of working for a People Pleaser, be active in looking out for the opportunities that will come your way to learn or which might leapfrog you ahead, such as:

- Good connections, in and around your organisation
- In a steady-state situation with no big changes looming and no misbehaving co-workers, a real sense of teamwork and together-ness that you can later replicate
- A focus on slow and steady incremental improvements that do add up over time.

On the minus side, what you probably won't get in your development on a People Pleaser's team and which you may want to actively look for elsewhere includes:

- How to spot usefully disruptive changes in organisations and industries
- How to tackle difficult conversations and hold people to account for the way they behave
- How to set and work towards ambitious, stretching goals.

Growth tips for People Pleasers

For those coaches, mentor-leaders and human resources professionals who want to help a People Pleaser to grow and develop, here are the factors that have proved most useful. I've given quite a bit of attention to confidence and to having difficult conversations, as working on just those two areas will usually make a big difference.

Mindset shifts around lack of confidence

Behind the warm and helpful nature of a People Pleaser there can sometimes be an unconscious lack of confidence. This is the place I would always start from in helping them to grow and develop. Having more confidence – and even just having more awareness about when their confidence is lacking – supports so many other possibilities. Here are the three steps to guide them through.

First, being aware of its impact

The impact in this context will be that a lack of confidence stops them from doing something that they know should be done. Ask if they have any awareness of the following patterns:

- They go to have a difficult conversation, and then find an excuse not to; or
- They put off implementing a big change; procrastinating and waiting for a time when they might feel strong enough to do it.

Second, being aware of their inner dialogue

Inner dialogue is the voice we use to talk to ourselves in our heads or sometimes the little whisper of self-doubt in our ears. I have given some examples here. The words in [square brackets] may vary depending on their situation.

Help them to recognise any inner dialogue they might be having that indicates a lack of confidence, perhaps along the lines of the following:

- *'I can't deal with that.'*
- *'I won't be able to do it.'*
- *'I'm not [tough] enough.'*
- *'If only I was more [decisive].'*

Third, taking action

For a lot of people, just knowing that everybody experiences this kind of lack of confidence from time to time, and becoming aware of how it impacts us if we let it, is enough to make a difference. At other times, once we have more awareness that a lack of confidence might exist, we might need to consciously choose what to do with that knowledge.

You can support a People Pleaser to move around and beyond their lack of confidence. Encourage them to get into **Action**, by helping them to consider:

- Overall, what's more important – their lack of confidence or the results of the action they need to take?
- Experimenting with small steps – so that they can learn what it's like to feel that their confidence isn't that strong – and to still take action on the tough thing anyway.
- Asking for support – almost everybody knows what it's like to not feel that confident and is often very happy to help.

Having difficult conversations

I started this chapter with this leadership quote:

> *'The standard you walk past becomes the standard you accept.'*

Research shows that all leaders need to set and maintain standards of behaviour for their teams so that they can be happy and effective. It isn't possible to let things go or to learn to tolerate bad behaviours even if tackling them is difficult. This just sets a new and lower standard, leading to an increase in what they'll then have to tolerate.

People Pleasers often find having that kind of conversation very difficult and it can help to have a framework of some kind. Here's the seven-point structure I normally use to coach my clients for a difficult conversation at work:

1 **Preparation** – get your facts together, decide what outcomes you want, and think ahead to what might happen.

2 **Location** – choose when and where to have the conversation. Usually somewhere quiet, private and free from distractions.

3 **Behaviours** – role model the behaviours you'd like to see: for example professional, composed, positive.

4 **Specific examples** – offer specific examples of problem behaviours or poor performance. Don't generalise and say 'You always do X' – be specific.

5 **Positive illustrations** – offer some guidance on what their behaviour or performance would look like in the future, once those issues have been successfully addressed.

6 **Plan** – agree on a plan of action for them; setting out what they will do, and when, and agree when you will next follow up.

7 **Support** – ask what they need to help make these changes successful and agree on what support you will provide.

Looking up and ahead

Once they've learned more about how their confidence functions and practised having those difficult conversations, People Pleasers then have a couple of important decisions to make about how they want to approach their work. Because of their interpersonal skills, they're usually pretty capable of doing these, but they might need some prompting to consider these important issues:

Step-changes

- How stable, really, is the department, organisation or industry that they are in?

- Is it possible for them to carry on incrementally improving things – or will some kind of step-change be needed sooner? Perhaps before someone else does it!

Contribution

- How happy are they with their contribution to the wider business?
- Do they want to influence the agenda more?
- Do they need to push their views a bit more confidently, to make the most of their strengths and connections?

Summary

- -

If a People Pleaser has become too difficult at work, there will probably be a simple paradox at the heart of the matter: you can't have a harmonious existence and manage to please everybody all of the time.

For leaders of a People Pleaser, their desire for everything to stay on a relatively even keel, with no major disruptions, can make them seem frustrating, slippery and less valuable than they should be. Leaders will need to make sure that their apparent agreement to a course of action isn't simply an expedient way of pleasing you, without any real intention to follow through. After that, focus your support on helping them to deal with the tough interpersonal issues that they'd rather avoid. Make sure that their well-developed relationship skills and connections are fully utilised for the business as a whole. And champion them, so that their self-effacing nature doesn't lead to them being overlooked.

Colleagues and team members of a People Pleaser can share some of the frustrations mentioned previously and may also suffer from their over-tolerance of poor behaviours or low standards. Colleagues should be alert to the risk of performance failures or project delays that might impact their joint work. Counter that risk with more active project management and a low tolerance for anything that's unsatisfactory. If you're a team member of a People Pleaser and somebody else on your team is not behaving well and isn't being held accountable for it, take steps to deal with this sooner rather than later, and seek support straight away. Both colleagues and team members can be proactive in asking for the help of a People Pleaser's wide network of connections.

Growth opportunities for a People Pleaser are likely to come from some solid work on their confidence, so they can recognise their strengths and not be so dependent on trying to keep everybody happy – and failing. Developing the skill of difficult conversations, and having a structure to help with this, will also make a big difference. Their sensitivity to other people and the ability this gives rise to in building and maintaining connections is powerful. They should decide if they want to use those skills more: to cope with step-changes rather than steady, incremental improvements; and to influence the wider business agenda more confidently.

If a People Pleaser can develop the confidence to disrupt things when occasionally necessary, they'll be able to unravel the paradox I mentioned earlier. That will lead them to the things they want from their work: happy people and well-performing teams around them; and the ability to guide and influence their organisation towards a steady future. That feels like a valuable win-win to me.

In the next chapter, we'll briefly look at some of the potentially difficult people who *aren't* in this book, including those who might 'Just want to watch the world burn'!

Note

1 Morrison, D (2022), 'Lieutenant General David Morrison AO' [YouTube Video], ICMI Speakers and Entertainers, Last retrieved 22 June 2023, from https://www.youtube.com/watch?v=s_TfZdIhIgg

chapter 19

Who's not here?

'No one can make you feel inferior
without your consent.'

Eleanor Roosevelt[1]

My first assignment with a really difficult client was a surprising one. The briefing I had received led me to expect a truly monstrous person – and that wasn't who I found. Instead, here was someone with a lot of responsibility, under a great deal of pressure, with some seriously inflexible approaches and some really self-defeating habits. These had combined to make life very difficult for the people around them.

Dealing with bad behaviour

Here in the UK we've recently seen reports about large public sector organisations, concluding that racism, sexism, homophobia and bullying are widespread.[2] If you even briefly scan the work-related sections of social media such as Reddit, you could conclude that those issues are endemic to all kinds of workplaces around the world, along with management and leadership that are either incompetent or in collusion.

Some of my commissions have been to support people who work for or alongside those who have become so difficult at work that their behaviour clearly falls into those categories. If that's you, the preceding chapters on the types of difficult people will be immediately helpful. Please make sure you don't wait too long, don't tolerate what is unacceptable and don't lose sight of your own power to change things. A few organisations are incredibly reluctant or slow to deal with these situations, even when they can. You must take steps in your own interests as soon as and as decisively as possible.

At the extreme

But I still wonder – what about those people at work who are behaving badly for other reasons? Not 'just' because they have entrenched habits and are under pressure, but because of something else?

For example, over the last ten years or so there has been a small rush of articles and books about personality disorders at work. People with a personality disorder that includes persistent patterns of manipulative, impulsive and antisocial behaviour, as well as a lack of empathy and remorse. You see less of those stories around now (perhaps because the reality is more nuanced) but some research indicated that up to 4 per cent of business leaders in the US might have such tendencies.[3]

However, other more recent research suggests that those old assumptions around ruthlessness and callousness being useful traits for business managers might be outdated.[4] That individuals with such traits seem able to 'talk the talk', but not 'walk the walk'. Perhaps implying that they are therefore not that successful at work in the longer term.

The key issue to note here is that I am not seeing people like those in my coaching practice. Because I don't have that experience (nor the kind of training required to identify, diagnose or treat them) they are not in this book.

But if people with severe personality disorders *are* still in the workplace, why am I not experiencing them?

It is probably for four good reasons:

1 Workplaces have already excluded them, using performance management processes.

2 Workplaces aren't investing in their development – and they are not coming to me privately.

3 I'm not spotting them. It's usually recognisable if clients are being manipulative and I'm often also working with data from colleagues and HR professionals about the impact people are having at work. But there must be the potential for me to miss some things.

4 They hold positions of authority in the workplace. And would not commission any kind of help that might lead to them having to change their behaviour.

For me, that last reason is the most troubling one, since it seems to be the point where the worst of the recent high-profile cases concerning abuse at work might have occurred. It also goes directly against my personal mission.

Compassionate and inclusive work

I'm about helping to make work a place where people want to join together to do things they couldn't do on their own. And, as a result, to satisfy fundamental human needs for meaning, fulfilment and belonging.

Because of my coaching work in the UK's National Health Service, I've been lucky enough to have coached several people who are right at the heart of providing care and treatment. Some of those clients care for people whose personality disorders might mean that they don't share those fundamental human needs in the same way that most of us do.

We must strive to make sure that people who need such care are getting it. That organisations are managed and led with compassion, equality and effectiveness. As individuals, we must exercise responsible agency and flexibility in how we look out for ourselves and relate to others. Those are things we can all do.

Next: the conclusion and summary to this book and some online resources to go further.

Notes

1 Roosevelt, Eleanor (1935). As cited in 'No one can make you feel inferior without your consent', Quote Investigator, April 2012. Last accessed 22 June 2023.

2 (a) 'Brits bearing the brunt of UK's bullying endemic.' *HR News*. 16 November 2022. Last accessed 22 June 2023; (b) 'Every fire brigade in England plagued by bullying and harassment claims, report finds'. *The Guardian*. 30 March 2023. Last accessed

22 June 2023; (c) 'Louise Casey's report on the Met police: the fall of a British institution.' *The Guardian.* 21 March 2023. Last accessed 22 June 2023.

3 Brown, Jessica. 'Do psychopaths really make better leaders?' BBC Worklife. 2 November 2017. Last accessed 22 June 2023.

4 Reece Akhtar, Gorkan Ahmetoglu, Tomas Chamorro-Premuzic, 'Greed is good? Assessing the relationship between entrepreneurship and subclinical psychopathy', *Science Direct: Personality and Individual Differences*, Volume 54, Issue 3, 2013.

chapter 20

———

In pursuit of a positive workplace

'Start by doing what's necessary;
then do what's possible; and suddenly
you are doing the impossible.'

Francis of Assisi[1]

As well as curiosity about why someone can seem so difficult and how working relationships might be improved, this book was partly born out of frustration and concern.

Frustration that leaders sometimes failed to tackle the obvious issues that can make a tough situation worse. Concern that colleagues of a difficult person were tolerating and suffering from the impacts. And that there weren't enough growth-focused interventions for those difficult people themselves.

A complex reality

In Part one of this book we saw that the reality behind those frustrations is more complex. In today's workplace, everybody is under some kind of pressure. Often outside their comfort zone, making tough choices, with a web of demanding relationships. The way we respond to those stresses, sometimes without enough consideration and sometimes inflexibly, is behind Chapter 3's perfect storm of why things can go wrong at work.

There's plenty of research to show that people don't leave jobs, they leave bad managers. That's a good reason for acting promptly when someone seems much too difficult at work. And there are other indications too. Chapter 4's warning signs help to make sense of what your intuition might already have been saying – that there's a difficult person at work and you need to take action.

Tools for change

Frameworks and structures like my Matrix of Difficult People in Chapter 5 can be useful in targeting what action to take. People respond differently to the same kinds of stress factors and focus their attention on different aspects of how to approach their work. That's why two people, alongside each other and under the same kind of pressure, can become difficult in quite different patterns. My Matrix and my Quick quiz help to identify those patterns and analyse what might be happening so that you can direct effective change.

The complexity and pace that we face at work means that as well as structure and framework, it's also useful to consider Chapter 8's Dynamic Principles. For example, to look for the positive intention behind someone's difficult behaviour, but also to balance that with knowledge of the actual impact it is having. And when we deal with difficult people to be kind, of course, but also to be fiercely committed to clear and respectful communication and well-established boundaries for behaviour.

Dealing with the nine types of difficult people

In Part two we considered each of my nine types in detail.

Scary Specialists value competence, drive and independence. And they demand equally high standards from those around them. To deal with a Scary Specialist, we need to reach through their tendency to disconnect from everything not up to their standard and demand that they develop new competencies. To become expert at working with others and not against them.

A **Dark Strategist** is compelled to figure out the keys to success. They will keep their distance and try to manoeuvre people like chess pieces. To deal with them, we need to get them much more engaged, in part by speaking their big-picture language. Enabling them to collaborate as well as strategise, and therefore deliver concrete progress as well as plans.

The **Martyr** buys into the myth of idealised outcomes and self-sacrifice. They will judge others who they believe to fall short of their high ideals. To tackle a Martyr we first need to win their trust by sticking to our own principles. And then help them learn to influence and compromise. So that a solution, even an imperfect one, is both achievable and sustainable.

A **Driving Force** is a resourceful, decisive and can-do person. They will be hugely intolerant of others who don't also seek out and meet challenges head on. To deal with a Driving Force we need to forcefully protect our boundaries, a stance they will respect. Then we can help them to value differences in approach. To become less bulldozer and more bridge-builder.

The **Revolutionary** is an enthusiastic person, readily embracing change and ideas. They will push for transformation regardless of consequences or consensus. Dealing with a Revolutionary is about finding common ground, avoiding burnout and isolation and getting the boring stuff done too. Show them that leading doesn't always mean going guerrilla.

Empire Builders are visionary charismatics, able to inspire people. They fear complexity and criticism and will seek to control the agenda rather than address those issues. Dealing with them means creating consensus, disagreeing safely, and helping them to overcome their fears and become more collegiate. Then they can build synergies rather than empires.

A **Worrier** is a conscientious, responsible and serious person. They will focus on the detail of what might go wrong – resulting in micromanagement and poor communication. Dealing with them needs affirmation, smoothing out relationships and a hard boundary against micromanaging. Then they can shift from being a terrier-like guard dog to a team-leading Labrador.

The **Rock** is a loyal, committed person. In the background, keeping things running. They will silently block anything they believe to be ill-conceived, even agreed priorities. We need to involve them more in decisions, especially around risks and consequences, and raise their horizons towards the bigger picture. This way, Rocks can become an enduring foundation.

People Pleasers are warm, self-effacing people with a network of trusted connections. They will avoid conflict and fail to contribute if doing so might rock the boat. Actively intervene with their over-tolerance of poor standards and help them feel confident about having tough conversations. By not always trying to please, they can create harmony and productivity.

My manifesto: fulfilling and effective workplaces

Work is important as it is such a huge part of our lives. If we get it right, it is where we can find meaning, fulfilment and connection. A difficult person at work is no exception to this. They're almost always somebody trying very hard to do what they see as the right thing, in the way that they know how. But if that's causing a problem then it's bad news all around. Because organisations can consistently deliver great products and services only when the people in them are effective and fulfilled.

We *can* deal with difficult people and quickly improve working relationships so that the game changes. When we balance those factors properly, work becomes a place where people can come together and support each other to achieve things that we can't do on our own. And then everybody benefits.

In the next chapter you'll find links to online and other resources to help identify and deal with difficult people and quickly improve working relationships.

Note

1 Assisi, Francis of (n.d.), as cited in 'Doing the impossible', Father Ed Dougherty, Catholic Review, 4 March 2021. Last accessed 22 June 2023.

chapter 21

Online and other resources

As you continue your journey to better understand and effectively deal with the nine types of difficult people, I've curated a set of resources to help. You'll find these at www.ninetypesofdifficultpeople.com

Each one is designed to enhance your ability to navigate challenging workplace interactions and further embed the strategies you've discovered in this book.

Next steps to deal with difficult people

1 **Companion Workbook and Flowchart:** This practical duo is a hands-on way to maximise your understanding and application of the book's concepts. They're designed to aid your navigation

through difficult workplace interactions. You can download them for free when you join my email list. Visit the website to access the 'Companion Workbook and Flowchart'.

2 **Interactive Quiz:** Interested in understanding the different types of difficult people you might be encountering at work? Visit my website and take the interactive quiz. You'll gain valuable insights to better navigate these challenging dynamics. Join my email list for access.

3 **One-to-One Executive Coaching**

- **For those dealing with difficult people:** Are you finding it challenging to handle a difficult person in your workplace? My one-to-one executive coaching can provide you with personalised strategies and techniques to effectively manage these challenging interactions. Reach out through the form on my website to discuss how this tailored approach can help you navigate your specific situation and create a more harmonious work environment.

- **For those perceived as difficult:** Do you find yourself in conflict at work, feel misunderstood by colleagues, or keep struggling to be heard and make progress? My one-to-one executive coaching can help. Together, we can explore the root of these challenges, work on your interpersonal skills, and devise strategies to improve your professional relationships. Contact me through the form on my website to discuss how this personalised coaching could assist in enhancing your communication, collaboration and success at work.

4 **Corporate Workshops:** Are you a team leader, HR professional or decision-maker looking to instil a more harmonious and pro-ductive work culture in your organisation? Consider my corporate workshops. These sessions, tailored to your specific needs, equip teams with practical skills for managing difficult individuals and situations, and enhancing interpersonal dynamics. Reach out through the form on my website to discuss the potential benefits for your organisation.

5 **Public Speaking Engagements:** Are you hosting a professional event or workplace seminar? I am available to bring my expertise to your audience. My talks focus on the strategies for dealing with difficult people in the workplace and fostering a positive work culture. Contact me through the form on my website to discuss potential speaking opportunities.

Expand your knowledge

1 **Monthly Webinars:** If you're interested in ongoing learning, consider subscribing to my monthly webinars. Each month, I'll explore various topics related to dealing with difficult individuals and fostering positive work relationships. Sign up for my email list to receive invitations to these insightful webinars.

2 **Blog and Vlog Posts:** Visit the website to explore a wealth of additional information in my blog and vlog posts. These resources provide timely, relevant insights and practical tips on managing workplace conflict and promoting a harmonious work environment.

3 **YouTube Channel:** For a more in-depth exploration of the book's themes and beyond, check out my YouTube channel. Here, I share strategies, ideas and personal experiences that complement and expand upon the material you've encountered in this book.

4 **Email Programme:** For regular insights and valuable tips delivered straight to your inbox, join my email programme. Over the course of several weeks, we'll delve deeper into the book's themes, share additional resources, and provide support as you work on improving your skills in dealing with difficult people at work.

Index